William Pugin Thornton

Phrenology, or, Heads, and what they tell us

William Pugin Thornton

Phrenology, or, Heads, and what they tell us

ISBN/EAN: 9783741155390

Manufactured in Europe, USA, Canada, Australia, Japa

Cover: Foto ©Andreas Hilbeck / pixelio.de

Manufactured and distributed by brebook publishing software
(www.brebook.com)

William Pugin Thornton

Phrenology, or, Heads, and what they tell us

MR. WILLIAM CULLEN BRYANT.
(Poet and Journalist.   Died June 12th, 1878.)

PHRENOLOGY

Heads, and What They Tell Us

BY

W. PUGIN THORNTON

ILLUSTRATED BY ELLEN WELBY

FOURTH THOUSAND

LONDON
SAMPSON LOW, MARSTON & COMPANY
Limited
St. Dunstan's House
FETTER LANE, FLEET STREET, E.C.
1896

PREFACE.

A FRIEND wishes me "to write something" explaining how it was I came to publish this work. We cannot often refuse an old friend's request, especially when, as in this instance, he has shown such an interest in one's writings that he has wished to christen them "Heads and Tales." I will, therefore, inflict a preface upon my readers, although I consider that it is a mistake to write one to so small a work.

In the latter part of 1889 I was asked to review a book on phrenology, and to further the writer's success as far as possible. Accordingly, I wrote an article for a monthly periodical, bringing forth the work in question. In consequence of something which occurred, my article never went out of my hands, but was put away, and almost forgotten, when a request came from my friends at the King's School in this town that I would lecture to the boys. The proposal was a trouble to me, as I dislike lecturing. What subject should I give, unless I made use of my phrenology manuscript? The subject fortunately was approved of, and I read the paper, or rather the greater portion of it, being called away to attend a sick person. Then came the thought of publishing the paper. Two periodicals refused it, and so I ventured to make "a shilling drefful" of my effort. I cannot but be glad that the little book has met with some success, for the first edition, published last August, consisted of five hundred copies, the second of one thousand.

I feel that the success of this book is greatly due to the excellence of the drawings, and I would, therefore, take this opportunity of thanking Miss E. Welby for her skilful efforts in what is a new sphere of work for her—phrenological sketching.

Phrenology being a personal study, I would apologize to all those the study of whose

heads I have made use of without asking
their permission.

No science satisfactorily gauges the functions of the brain. Anthropologists (ἄνθρωπος
a man, and λόγος discourse) have of late
years occupied themselves much concerning the outside and inside measurement of
skulls. They have arranged skulls in the
general orders of Dolichocephalic (long-
headed), Brachicephalic (short-headed),
Stenocephalic (narrow-headed), Eurocephalic
(broad-headed). Those skulls which are remarkable for neither length nor shortness are
called Orthocephalic, or, as Professor Flower,
late Conservator of the College of Surgeons
Museum, and other members of the Anthropological Institute, term them Mesocephalic.
Anthropologists agree that the size and
shape of the skull coincide with the size and
shape of its brain; and, further, that the
brain is the organ of the mind. But Anthropologists have not found that any particular
mental characteristics are specially connected with the length, breadth, or shortness of skulls either amongst various nations,

or amongst individuals. Therefore the classi-
fications dolicocephalic, brachicephalic, &c.,
are of little value, except for anthropological
purposes.

Pathological observations, owing to the
comparatively small amount of localized
injuries and diseases of the brain, are scanty.
Experimental physiology discovers but little
else than the nervous centres for the various
muscular movements of the body, limbs, and
organs, and consequently is only of value,
and of great value, in localizing disease, or
in the application of surgical operations on
the brain. Phrenology is nothing more than
a method of observing by the eye or by the
touch projections or depressions on the outside of the skull, which denote an unusual
size or a diminution of the convolutions of
the brain lying immediately underneath. To
make the study of the functions of the brain
more perfect, the four sciences, anatomy,
pathology, physiology, and phrenology, will
have to be taken conjointly.* I believe

* On the eve of sending the manuscript to the
publishers, I came across the following sentence of

when that is done the truest results will be obtained.

.W. P. T.

Canterbury, April 23rd, 1892.

Professor Ferrier's in his address before the Anthropological Institute, February 22nd, 1887, on " How far recent investigations on the functional topography of the brain could be brought in relation with craniological and anthropological researches with a view to establish the foundations of a scientific phrenology." Dr. Ferrier said, "That the data of a scientific phrenology were, as yet, very deficient ; but there was reason to believe that, if the subject were taken up from different points of view by the anatomist, physiologist, psychologist, and anthropologist, great progress might be made." I am very glad to find that Professor Ferrier and myself are not at enmity on the subject of phrenology. I thought, judging from the second edition of his work (1886), referred to later on, that we were at serious loggerheads.

HEADS, AND WHAT THEY TELL US.

~~~~~~~~~~

THE word "Phrenology" is not found in Walker's Dictionary of 1830, but later lexicographers tell us that it means "the science of the human mind." The name was given to the Science by Dr. Thomas Forster in 1816. Mr. Easy, the father of our old friend "Mr. Midshipman Easy," appears, as we read in Captain Marryat's tale, to have considered himself fully acquainted with the science. In choosing a foster-nurse for Master Easy, the following conversation takes place :

"I have examined her," replied the doctor, "and can safely recommend her."

"That examination is only preliminary to one more important," replied Mr. Easy. "I must examine her."

" Examine who, Mr. Easy?" exclaimed his wife, who has lain down again on the bed.

" The nurse, my dear."

" Examine what, Mr. Easy?" continued the lady.

" Her head, my dear," replied her husband. " I must ascertain what her propensities are."

" I think you had better leave her alone, Mr. Easy. She comes this evening, and I shall question her pretty severely. Dr. Middleton, what do you know of this young person?"

" I know, madam, that she is very healthy and strong, or I should not have selected her."

" But is her character good?"

" Really, madam, I know little about her character, but you can make any inquiries you please. But at the same time I ought to observe, that if you are too particular on that point you will have some difficulty in providing yourself."

" Well, I shall see," replied Mrs. Easy.

" And I shall feel," rejoined the husband.

This parleying was interrupted by the arrival of the very person in question, who was announced by the housemaid, and was ushered in. She was a handsome, florid, healthy-looking girl, awkward and naïve in her manner, and apparently not over wise; there was more of the dove than of the serpent in her composition.

Mr. Easy, who was very anxious to make his own discoveries, was the first who spoke. " Young woman, come this way; I wish to examine your head."

" Oh! dear me, sir, it's quite clean, I assure you," cried the girl, dropping a curtsey.

Dr. Middleton, who sat between the bed and Mr. Easy's chair, rubbed his hands and laughed.

In the meantime, Mr. Easy had untied the string and taken off the cap of the young woman, and was very busy putting his fingers through her hair, during which the face of the young woman expressed fear and astonishment.

" I am glad to perceive that you have a large portion of benevolence."

"Yes," replied the young woman, dropping a curtsey.

"And veneration also."

"Thankee, sir."

"And the organ of modesty* is strongly developed."

"Yes, sir," replied the girl, with a smile.

"That's quite a new organ," thought Dr. Middleton.

"Philo-progenitiveness† very powerful."

* A "bump" unknown in phrenology.

† Fondness for children and animals, situated at the back of the head. Philo-progenitiveness is a compound of the Greek and English words φίλος (love of) and Progeny, and was called by Gall, Amour de la progeniture. This faculty is distinct from Amativeness, which Gall named, Instinct de la generation, de la reproduction ; instinct de la propagation ; instinct vénérien ; and which he placed below Philo-progenitiveness, at the junction of the head with the neck, which would be in the portion of the brain called the Cerebellum. Professor Ferrier, in his second edition of "Functions of the Brain," writes concerning this faculty, "I do not consider it necessary to discuss the most widely known but least well founded of all the hypotheses as to the functions of the cerebellum, viz. that of Gall, which regards this organ as the seat of sexual instinct." On the other hand, cases of disease and injury to this portion of the brain, with consequent loss of the instinct, have been reported.

PHILO-PROGENITIVENESS,

"If you please, sir, I don't know what that is," answered Sarah, with a curtsey.

"Nevertheless, you have given us a practical illustration. Mrs. Easy, I am satisfied. Have you any questions to ask? But it is quite unnecessary."

"To be sure I have, Mr. Easy. . . ."

We may remember how, later in life, poor Mr. Easy, in his study of phrenology, had the temerity to try to alter the bumps on his head by a machine he had invented, and how, in his contest with the science, he died a martyr to his foolishness.

Phrenology was much in vogue forty to seventy years ago, but it lost in favour with the public because of the extravagant behaviour of many of its adherents. Captain Marryat justly caricatured them in his novel.

If, too, we remember the story told by Lord Macaulay, we cannot be surprised that sensible people should have become disgusted with phrenology. Macaulay, after returning with Lord Aberdeen and Sir George Grey by train from a visit to the Queen at Windsor in 1851, wrote in his diary: "Jan. 16.—We

B

talked much together till another party got into the carriage; a canting fellow and a canting woman. Their cant was not religious, but philanthropical and phrenological. I never heard such stuff. It was all that we could do to avoid laughing out loud. The lady pronounced that the Exhibition of 1851 would enlarge her ideality, and exercise her locality."

That phrenology should have been put aside is regrettable, for it is a true science, reasonable in its facts, and not a quackery.

That there is intimate relation between phrenology, as first expounded at the end of the last century by the learned French physician Dr. Gall, and the functions of the brain, there can be no doubt to those who have studied the subject.

Unfortunately, physiologists are not able to experiment upon human beings, because none of our fellow-men have been kind enough to allow portions of their skulls to be removed in order that certain points on their brain surfaces might be tickled, or slices of the convolutions taken away. If such

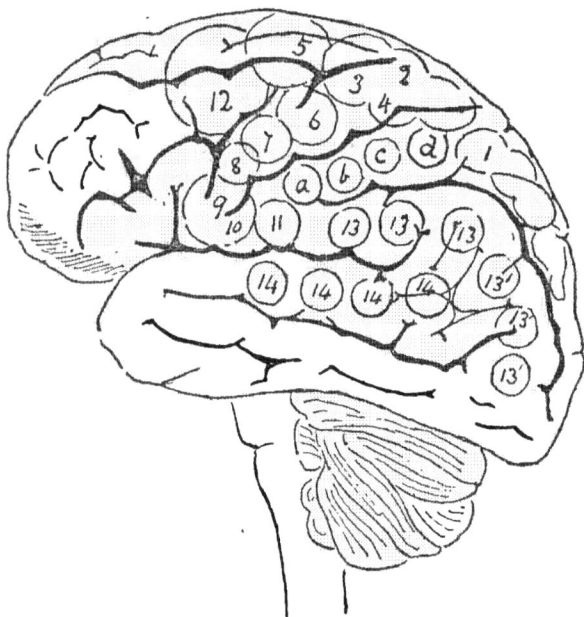

VIEW OF LEFT SIDE OF HUMAN BRAIN.
(Copied from Fig. 130 in Professor Ferrier's second edition of
"The Functions of the Brain, 1886.")

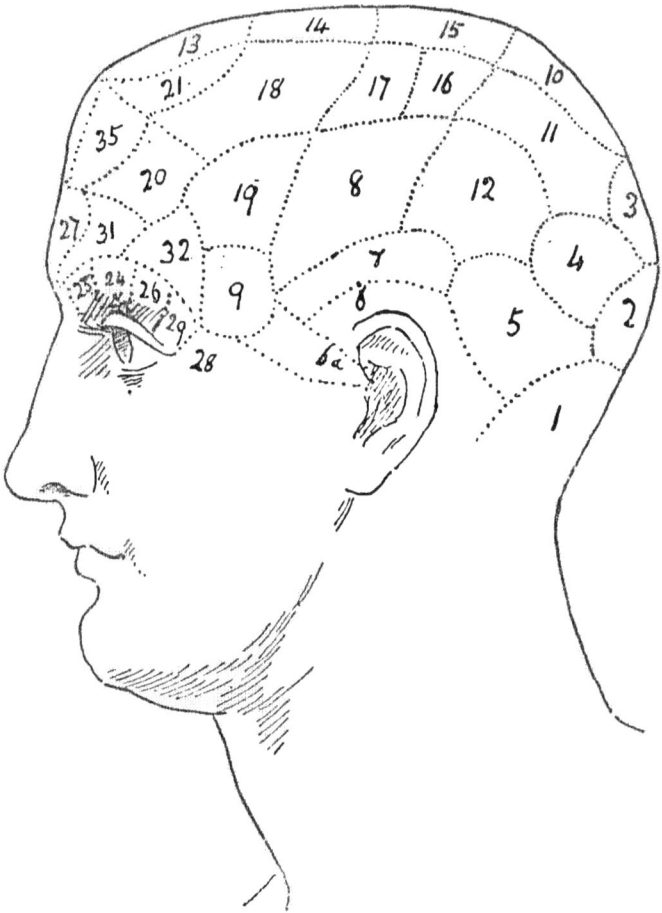

A PHRENOLOGICAL DRAWING OF THE LEFT SIDE OF THE HEAD
(Copied from Mr. George Combe's "Elements of
Phrenology, 1843.")

experiments had been made, especially of the latter kind, and the results tabulated, then many, if not all, of the functions of the brain, which have been localized by Gall and other phrenologists, would probably have been verified. Up to the present time experimental brain physiology has only extended to cats, dogs, monkeys, &c., which animals possess but few of the higher mental attributes of man. Therefore the result of physiologists' experiments must necessarily fall short of what it should be.

To prove that the areas of physiological research and the areas of phrenological research differ little either numerically or in their positions, it is only necessary to compare the two accompanying drawings. The first one is a view of the left side of the human brain. The second drawing is a view of the left side of a man's head. In both the areas are mapped out and numbered. It will be noted that there are no areas marked in the front part of the drawing of the brain, which portion is called, later on, the frontal lobe; nor again, in the hinder shaded portion,

called Cerebellum. But it will be seen that
in the drawing of the head both the forepart
and the hinderpart are mapped out. This
is a reason why the figures on the drawing
of the head are more numerous than those
on the drawing of the brain. With this
distinction it can be said that the areas
mapped out by physiologists are about the
same in number as those mapped out by
phrenologists. Each area marked by the
phrenologist covers, undoubtedly, a convolution of the brain, and every convolution is
supposed, both by the physiologist and the
phrenologist, to be the centre of a special
action or faculty. And therefore, looking
broadly at the efforts of such physicians as
Dr. Ferrier, the well-known brain physiologist, and Dr. Gall, who was a great dissector
of brains as well as a phrenologist, we may,
in one sense, say that they have worked on
a common basis; at any rate, it should not
be said that the multitude of mappings out
on the skull by the phrenologist must of
necessity be ridiculous, for if it were so,
then the numerous marked areas of the
physiologist are worthy of ridicule.

The dark, irregular lines in the drawing of the brain represent the fissures which run between the convolutions of the brain. The circles with letters and numbers have reference to the annexed table, which, taken from Professor Ferrier's previously-mentioned work, gives the results of electrical brain experiments on a monkey.

The lower portion, shaded with fine lines, is the cerebellum (see foot-note, page 14).

"1. The opposite hind-leg is advanced as in walking.

"2. Flexion with outward rotation of the thigh, rotation inwards of the leg with flexion of the toes.

"3. Similar to Nos. 1 and 2. Sometimes the tail moved.

"4. The opposite arm is adducted, extended, and retracted, the hand pronated.

"5. Extension forwards of the opposite arm.

"*a. b. c. d.* Clenching of the fist.

"6. Flexion and supination of the forearm.

"7. Retraction and elevation of the angle of the mouth.

"8. Elevation of the ala of the nose and upper lip.

"9 and 10. Opening of the mouth with protrusion (9) and retraction (10) of the tongue.

"11. Retraction of the angle of the mouth.

"12. The eyes open widely, the pupils dilate, and head and eyes turn to the opposite side.

"As a rule, stimulation of the frontal lobes, which

are in advance of 12, as well as the orbital lobale, was without obvious effect.

"13 and 13'. The eyes move to the opposite side.

"14. Pricking of the opposite ear, head and eyes turn to the opposite side, pupils dilate widely."

The figures in the drawing of the phrenological head represent the following faculties:—

1. Amativeness.	16. Conscientiousness.
2. Philoprogenitiveness.	17. Hope.
3. Concentrativeness.	18. Wonder.
4. Adhesiveness.	19. Ideality.
5. Combativeness.	20. Wit.
6. Destructiveness.	21. Imitation.
6a. Alimentiveness.	23. Form.
7. Secretiveness.	24. Size.
8. Acquisitiveness.	26. Colouring.
9. Constructiveness.	27. Locality.
10. Self-esteem.	28. Number.
11. Love of approbation.	29. Order.
12. Cautiousness.	31. Time.
13. Benevolence.	32. Tune.
14. Veneration.	35. Causality.
15. Firmness.	

A few of the centres for certain functions have been located by physiologists in the brain over which corresponding phrenological bumps have been marked on the skull. Thus it has been pointed out that the brain centre for movements of the face muscles lies under Imitation (Gall's Faculté d'imiter, mimique). The centre of concentration of attention (13) lies under Concentrativeness (3); the gustatory centre (9) under Alimentiveness (6*a*) or the Organ of the Appetite for Food. The brain area for speech (Broca's convolution, or the posterior extremity of the third frontal convolution), which has been found by Dr. Broca in consequence of the effects of injury and disease, lies under that region of the skull on which is marked Language. Dr. Hollander read a paper on this subject before the Anthropological Institute, February 12th, 1889. When Dr. Gall was a boy at school he first noticed that there was a connection between prominent eyes and verbal memory, for his schoolfellows who learnt easily by heart had prominent eyes. These boys were nick-named "Jeux de bœuf," or "ox-eyed." With the cause of that prominence he was then unacquainted, but afterwards ascertained it to be the predominant size of a certain convolution of the brain, which, by pressing on the hinder part of the roof of the orbit, pushed the eye outwards. This was the first observation which led this youthful genius (then nine years of age) to seek for external signs of the mental faculties.

Another incident in his school-life Gall relates which led him later on to determine the position of Locality. He was fond of birdnesting and taking birds with snares, but he always had great difficulty in finding the trees he had marked and the snares he had set. One of his schoolfellows, however, could find the places without any hesitation, although he was a youth of only moderate abilities. Gall took a cast of his head, and later in life was able to place it side by side with casts of the heads of two men who both had a facility for finding or recalling to mind places they had once seen. Comparison was Gall's principal method for finding out the truth of phrenology. Gall found that, although these three casts differed in many respects, they all had an enlargement immediately above the eyes on each side of the root of the nose. Subsequent observations confirmed this position as that of Locality.

I will not enter into any particulars of the close connection between phrenological bumps and the convolutions of the brain, but having enjoyed a knowledge of phrenology for more than twelve years, I will make some observations on my general acquaintance with this science, at the same time noting some of the incidents in connection with it.

In 1878 I became acquainted with Major Noel, who was an enthusiastic phrenologist. He had lived for many years in Vienna, and during that time had published works on phrenology. Under his guidance I commenced the study of the science, and ever since have kept it up, often finding it a source of amusement, and not infrequently of good service to me.

It is to the late Major Noel's kindness that I am indebted for possessing the published works of Gall, Spurzheim, Combe (a gift of Mr. George Combe's in 1843 to Major Noel), and others. Major Noel would have

also given me his collection of casts of heads
had not his nephew, Lord Wentworth, had
the first claim upon them ; a circumstance
I would say, perhaps selfishly but in all
humbleness of spirit, I much regretted.

Phrenology gives a direct and immediate
insight into the character of men, if seen, of
course, with their heads uncovered. It is
by no means necessary that a man should
be bald, although baldness is of assistance
in gaining an idea of the shape of a head.
Baldness also enables one better to note the
presence or absence of some small phrenological eminences, as, for instance, Firmness.

It is not so easy to estimate female character, because ladies' present style of doing
their hair prevents a full appreciation of the
shape of their heads ; and this statement
is readily proved by making a comparison,
which we may be excused for doing, between
the portrait of Her Majesty, by Sir W.
C. Ross, R.A., in 1841, and the one of the
Princess of Wales, recently by Van der
Weyde, both here reproduced from the
Graphic.

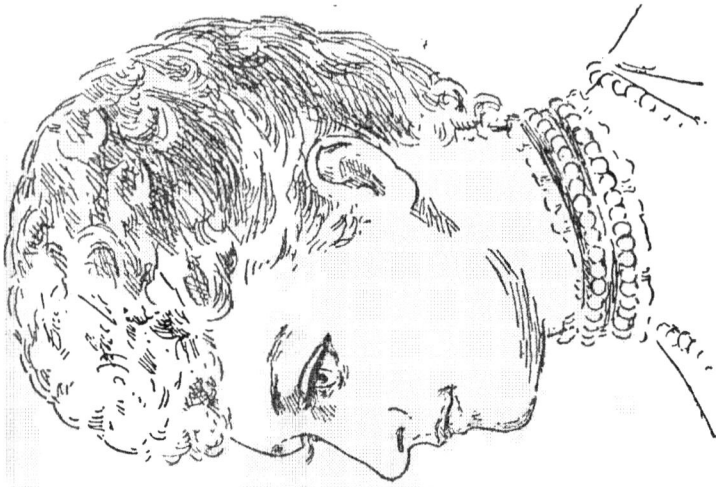

H.R.H. THE PRINCESS OF WALES.

H.M. THE QUEEN.

(From the *Graphic*, Nov. 7, 1891.)

DEPRESSED ACROSS THE CENTRE.

Generally after meeting a man for the first time, one tries to prove if his general behaviour agree with his phrenological character, but should there not be this opportunity, one has learnt to be satisfied with a phrenological estimate of his character ; and this is because anyone understanding phrenology finds that the shape of a man's head and his character never greatly disagree. There may be variations, due to his manner of bringing up and to his degree of education, or there may be differences between the phreno-logical inference and his character, as it is when such excess as drink or living beyond his means has beset the man.

Speaking broadly, a phrenologist is at once ready to trust a man should the crown portion of his head be well raised, as seen in the frontispiece; but if, on the other hand, the top of the man's head be flat, or depressed across the centre, then phreno-logical knowledge should step in, and one should hesitate as to trusting that man too readily.

The accompanying drawing shows absence

of the bump of Veneration as well as that
of Conscientiousness. Conscientiousness lies
immediately below the hollowed central portion of the crown, Veneration being situated
in the crown.

To give an instance of my meaning, I will
relate an incident which happened about ten
years ago. I was travelling on the Under-
ground Railway in London with my friend
Mr. Byam, of Chester Square. At Padding-
ton Station a well-dressed man entered the
carriage. On sitting down he removed his
hat, showing a head much depressed in the
centre. My friend, having himself, at that
time, no knowledge of phrenology, but well
knowing my regard for it, asked me what I
thought of our neighbour's head. I whispered
back, " Travelling with a third-class ticket."
At Baker Street Station a ticket inspector
appeared at the window and asked for our
tickets. We showed ours, but our fellow-
traveller was immediately seized with an
excessive anxiety to find his. He felt in his
waistcoat pockets, he felt in his trousers
pockets, then in the breast pockets of his

coat, then back to his waistcoat pockets, muttering all the time about the curious way in which he had mislaid his ticket. The inspector evidently appreciated the man's dilemma, for he said, " I don't think you'll be able to find it," and coming into the carriage he wrote him out a ticket whilst the train went on, charging our traveller first-class fare from the terminus station. It was a conundrum. Which pocket held his third-class ticket? Certainly not either of the breast pockets of his coat, though his over-zealousness made him feel in them.

One of our illustrated comic papers used in former days frequently to picture a well-known character with a head possessing a good vault, otherwise called the crown. This falsity of draughtsmanship became so much an annoyance to me that I wrote to the editor, and I am glad to say the paper's artist took my advice, and always afterwards represented this head as flat at the top, as the photographs exhibited in shop windows showed it to be.

Artists, of all people, should have an

acquaintance with phrenology, especially
artists who draw for illustrated papers,
portraying heads of every-day life.

There was a sale of the Duke of Hamilton's
pictures some years ago—I mean the one in
which a most exquisite painting of Hobbema's,
a woodland scene, was sold for 4500*l.*
Amongst this collection was the portrait of
an unnamed saint. Sad to relate, the saint
had a most unsaintly head; so flat at the
top that I instinctively felt the man must
rather have been a sinner, at any rate not
the man whose head qualified him to be por-
trayed as a saint. Evidently the artist knew
nothing of phrenology, or, if he were
acquainted with the science, he had to paint
the man's portrait against his wish, and thus
took his revenge. I well remember coming
suddenly upon this picture, as I turned
to the left from the doorway of one of the
inner rooms at Messrs. Christie and Manson's,
and astonishing the friend who was with me
by laughing when he read out the picture's
title in the catalogue. I have often won-
dered who secured that portrait of my un-

saintly saint, which, in my estimation, without its frame, was worth about twopence.

It has been recognized at Scotland Yard that the position of the ears of habitual criminals is very often low down on the head.

Taking a straight line from the outer corner of the eye towards the back of the head, the opening of the ear in most cases is found to be a little below this line. Those who have the centres of their ears in the same straight lines as the corners of their eyes (see drawing "Fore-half large" on page 91) will be found to be of quiet dispositions, not inclined to wage war with their neighbours, though perhaps much provoked by them. Those whose ears lie very much below the straight line are those who, as it has been before mentioned, are not unlikely to come under the notice of the police authorities. The explanation of this variation in the position of the ears is due to the amount of those qualities known in phrenology as the animal propensities. When there is a large amount of one, or all, of the qualities—Destructiveness (Gall's Instinct carnassier; penchant au meurtre), Secretiveness (Gall's Ruse ; finesse ; savoir-faire), Acquisitiveness (Gall's Sentiment de la propriété ; instinct de faire des provisions ; couvoitise ; perchant au vol), Combativeness (Gall's Instinct de la défense de soi-même et de sa propriété; penchant aux rixes; courage), then the ear is noticed to be in a position lower than is usually seen (see drawing " Back-Half large " on page 93).

It must be noted, however, that to be a phrenological criminal, one should be deficient in that portion of the head which contains the good qualities, which will be mentioned later on, and which qualities leaven the whole malice of one's nature.

The most marked case of a low-pitched ear that I have ever met with was at one of the Lewes Assizes. A boy of ten years was brought up on account of his continually thieving from tills. His father, a most respectable-looking mechanic, who had charge of him in the dock, said that his son had been deaf and dumb from birth ; that he had done all he could to keep him out of

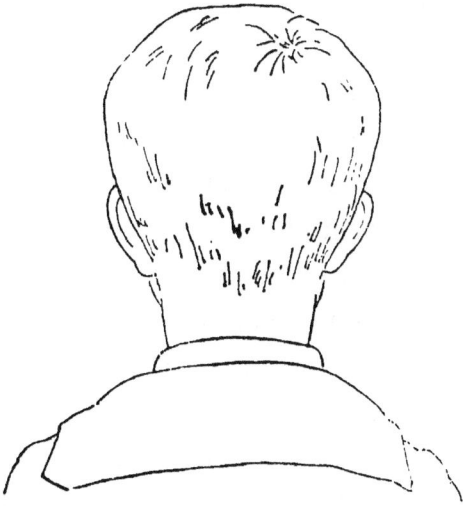

CAUTIOUSNESS.
(Master Edmund Skinner.)

harm, but that he found the boy utterly beyond his control; and that he would be much obliged if the judge would send him for a long term of imprisonment, so as to save him from becoming an habitual criminal. The boy's ears were so low that they seemed, in the distance, to grow out of his neck. This case undoubtedly supported the truth of phrenology. Here we had a boy who, although afflicted with two notable infirmities, deafness and dumbness, was an active thief, and one who would be a thief, do what his father could to stop him.

The "bumps" of Cautiousness (Gall's Circonspection; prévoyance), situated at the upper part of the sides of the back portion of the head, are often met with. They always bear testimony to the correctness of Dr. Gall's discovery, and their absence also proves his rule.

A friend of mine, an army surgeon, has told me, on my remarking that his son had this shape of head (the drawing is taken from the boy), that this little fellow of four years of age always made his younger brother go first over any place he thought was not safe; and that this habit was not his only qualification for cautiousness.

The enlargement at each side of the head, known as Constructiveness (Gall's Sens de mécanique; sens de construction; talent de l'architecture), lying about mid-distance between the eye and the ear, but on a higher level, is not uncommon. The most striking instances I can bring to mind are the following. When I was practising in London as a surgeon, a boy of eight years of age was brought to me by his mother. I was at once struck with the unusual development of this boy's bumps of Constructiveness, and I asked him if he was fond of cutting out things. The mother at once answered for him, " Oh! yes. He is always making us pieces of furniture with any bit of wood he can get hold of."

A gentleman, who was some years ago with me on the Committee of the St. Marylebone General Dispensary, London, mentioned that he was dissatisfied with the way in which his son was being taught at school, and that the following day he was going out to the school to decide if he should remove his boy. He asked me if I would go with him. I accompanied my friend, and on being introduced to the master of the school, was so struck with his large developments of Constructiveness, that I hazarded the question, with an apology, Whether he was an inventor? His answer was : " What makes you ask that? But come with me and see." We followed him to an upper room, and there, in construction, was a large machine, which he explained was for turning esparto grass into paper, and he was hoping soon to perfect it in order to claim the Government reward of, I believe, 20,000*l.* for such an invention. The time he gave to his pet scheme was, my friend thought, so much less time for teaching his son; but he may have been wrong.

When living in London I became acquainted with a doctor residing in Prince's Street, Cavendish Square. This gentleman, whose name I forget, had the bumps of Constructiveness very fully developed. He told me that his constant desire to invent

something was a bother to him, that he was
sure he spent too much time over such work.
He showed me an admirable invalid bed, also
a circular seat for placing, unassisted, an
invalid, who was perfectly helpless, on to a
bed.   This, too, was ingenious, and evidently
of great use.   One story he told was very
amusing.   When he was practising in the
country some years before, he found himself one day called in to see a person
suddenly taken ill.   He was four miles from
home and without instruments.   An idea
struck him, and he asked for an umbrella.
They brought him one.   " No, not that kind ;
one of the old gamp sort, I want."   There
happened to be one in the house, and having
obtained leave to do what he liked with Mrs.
Gamp, he cut out one of the whalebone ribs,
which he soon fashioned to his requirements.
He was shortly after able to leave the house,
having entirely relieved his patient.   He
told me it was afterwards the saying, in that
part of the country, that he had performed
an operation with an umbrella.

In 1883 I twice attended the Chess Tournament, held at the Criterion, not so much for the purpose of watching the games as for noting if there was any peculiar configuration of heads amongst the players. As the following letter explains itself, I will here make use of it, for having been written to the editor of the *Jewish Chronicle*, it has had but a limited circulation:—

"London, July 9th, 1883.

"SIR,—In the *Standard* of Saturday last I read an extract from your journal, in which was stated the interesting fact that a large proportion of the players in the Chess Tournament were Jews, and, moreover, that these players carried off half the prizes, securing the first and second places in the list of eight winners. The extract pointed out that the pre-eminence of the Jews in the game was undoubtedly due to the well-known qualities of the Jewish race, namely the mathematical bent of mind, the patience, the perseverance, the daring, and, lastly, the peculiar quality known as long-headedness. It is to the commonly-used expression 'long-headedness' that I would draw attention, and would briefly show how erroneously the term is used if it is meant to betoken a man's mental qualities by the shape of his head.

" During the time of the tournament I paid a visit to the Criterion for the special purpose of noting if there was any formation of the head at all common to chess-players. I soon found that many possessed a greater breadth of head than is usually seen in that portion which lies above a line drawn from the top of the ears to the eyebrows, where phrenologists place 'constructiveness,' and I noted that this shape of head was present mostly in those players who I now learn from your paper were Jews. This preponderating width of head was most noticeable in Dr. Zukertort. I did not notice that any of the players were particularly long-headed.

" The late Major Noel, a most correct and moderate expounder of phrenology, has written in his work, ' On the Physical Basis of Mental Life' (1873, Longmans), as follows : ' The classification of heads, however, as dolicocephalic and brachicephalic (long heads

CONSTRUCTIVENESS.

Dr. Zukertort.   Copied from a photograph (taken in 1868) by
the kind permission of the proprietor of Simpson'sChess
Divan.)

D

and short heads), throws but little light on the character of races, and still less on the dispositions and capabilities of individuals. . . . I have known some long-headed men to be very stupid, and others to be very clever, and have gained similar experiences in regard to short heads.'

" It can be readily understood how such a quality as ' constructiveness '—which may be termed in this case 'planning out'— would prove of immense value in a game of chess. Given this quality in profusion, it would seem that there is little need for a player to be endued with more than an ordinary amount of intellectual qualities in order to prove himself a brilliant player."

The most intellectually shaped head I noticed amongst those chess-players was that of Mr. Bird.

The observation made by the late Major Noel on the classification of heads, and one's own acquaintance with the subject, tend to shake belief in the value of Mr. Havelock Ellis's remarks on the heads of criminals in his otherwise sensible and justly written

work, " The Criminal " (1890). He writes,
" All the cranial abnormalities are found
occasionally in ordinary persons ; very rarely
are they found combined in normal persons to
the extent that they are found among instinc-
tive criminals. Thus Lombroso " (an Italian
writer on prison life), " when he examined
the skull of Gasparone, a famous brigand of
the beginning of the century, whose name
still lives in legends and poems, found
microcephaly * of the frontal region, a
wormian† bone, eurigmatism,‡ increase in
the orbital capacity, oxycephaly,§ and ex-

* Of a small or imperfectly-formed skull.

† Small bones of the skull named after the anatomist
Wormius.

‡ Although I have had the kind assistance of Mr. J. B.
Bailey, the eminent librarian of the College of Surgeons,
I have been unable to find this word. It is not in
Thomas's Medical Dictionary of 1886, nor in Billings's
of 1890, nor in Whitney's very recent Century Dictionary ;
and I cannot trace it from any Greek word.

§ Early union of the spaces between the side and back
bones of the skull by bone, with consequent development
of the membranous spaces between the front bones of the
skull. This condition of early life gives the head a pointed
appearance, and questionably has been said, by impeding
development of the brain, to produce cretinism.

SELF-ESTEEM.

The side view of this head is, after the manner of prison photography, shown by means of a looking-glass.)

treme dolichocephaly." *   Such a classification of a head throws but little light, as
Major Noel would have said, on the disposi-
tion and capability of an individual. The
language, to make use of another long word
which appears, though in another sense, in
the same paragraph as the sentences I have
above quoted, is teratologic.†   The titles
used in phrenology, though mostly of great
length, are, however, "understandable of
the people," for with the exception of Philo-
progenitiveness they are, as for instance,
Cautiousness and Concentrativeness, only
compound English words.

Self-esteem (Gall's Orgueil; hauteur; fierté;
amour de l'autorité; elevation) is undoubtedly
a true faculty; as pointed out by Gall it is
seen as a tilting up of the back of the crown
of the head. It certainly is an objectionable
quality except to the owner, whom it perhaps helps in his business or profession,
making his customers, clients or patients,

* Longheadedness.
† As the Americans say "tall."   In Mr. Ellis's meaning, "a monstrosity."

believe that he is a better man than he is.
It is, therefore, especially useful to a man
with a small head.

It is often noted that a man who has the
bump of Self-esteem walks in a manner
which bears testimony to the truth of phrenology, for his gait is characteristic of his
presumed superiority.   His brain guides his
footsteps.

As surgeon to one of Her Majesty's prisons
I have at times to make a general inspection
of the prisoners.   It is then I am often im-
pressed by the fact that Self-esteem is
present to a larger extent amongst criminals
than it would be amongst a similar number
of ordinary individuals.

Firmness (Gall's Fermeté; constance; perseverance; opiniâtreté) is betokened by a small
eminence at the back of the top of the head
in front of Self-esteem, in the position
pictured in the drawing.   I possess this
bump, and my family pleasantly term it
" obstinacy "—but obstinacy and firmness
are two different qualities, I am glad to say.

Gall says, " La fermeté et l'opiniâtreté

FIRMNESS.

découlent de la même source. L'homme borné, l'enfant, sont entêtés, intraitables ; l'homme raisonnable est constant, inébranlable, persévérant, ferme."

There is one more special development to which I would refer before finishing these personal proofs of the value of phrenology : it is the heaviness of the upper eyelids on their outer side, immediately under the eyebrows. This fulness denotes Language. Gall divided the faculty into two divisions, one expressed by Sens du Langage, de parole, Talent de la philologie ; the other by Sens des mots, Sens des noms, Mémoire des mots, mémoire verbale. The faculty, I believe, can reasonably be separated into two parts, at the same time they are often associated in the same person. We will therefore understand the faculty to signify " Language " and " Verbal memory." Language is found with all natural orators, its absence denoting the reverse. I will give an example which came under my observation. Some years ago I was dining at an Old Wykehamist Dinner. We had been listening to speeches from **Dr.** Ridding, now the Bishop of Southwell, who was in the chair, and from Lord Selborne, neither of whom has the Language enlargement. Sitting next to an old schoolfellow, Canon William Awdry of Chichester, I remarked to him, as one present about five seats from us rose to speak, "Now we shall hear somebody who has the gift of the gab." "Don't you know who that is ?" said my neighbour ; " why, it is Borlase, Member for East Cornwall. He was at school with us." I had not recognized him, but my remark that he had the gift of language immediately proved itself true, for our old schoolfellow, taking up the book of the songs, began on that theme, and for quite twenty minutes kept us listening to a flow of words.

Language is a most enviable faculty, one to which I myself can lay no iota of claim, sometimes much to my regret and annoyance. It is, however, a quality which should be backed by a good brain, *i.e.* a well-developed head, or its owner will earn the titles I have heard given, "irresponsible"

LANGUAGE

WITHOUT LANGUAGE.

and " irrepressible." At any rate, Language is a faculty undoubtedly very difficult to keep in abeyance.

Whoever has heard the late and greatly lamented Archbishop of York and Sir James Paget has had difficulty in deciding which of these highly intellectual men was the most powerful speaker. Dr. Magee, in the debate in the House of Lords on the Irish Church Disestablishment Bill in 1864, and the Cathedrals Bill in 1883, must have been grand to listen to. Sir James Paget, I know myself, was unsurpassable in his speeches at the London Medical Congress in 1881, where, before foreign and English audiences, he so worked up the mental fervour of his listeners by the perfect beauty and power of his language, that at the termination of his addresses it was evident that every one was, for the time, lost in admiration of the superb speaker.

A phrenologist would say that the speeches of the former were the effort of natural oratory, and those of the latter the outcome of well-studied exercise.

E

And so it is with Mr. Henry Dickens, Q.C., of the South-Eastern Circuit. I trust my friend will excuse the unfortunate personality of phrenology when I state that it tells that he is not a natural orator, but that his great power of speech so often shown in addressing juries is also the outcome of well-studied exercise, associated with his perfect constructive management of his cases.

Verbal Memory is shown by a prominent eye, an eye in which a large amount of the white portion is seen. As noticed on page 27, it was the association of these two conditions of body and mind which led Gall as a boy to first think of phrenology. The prominence of the eye which is present in the disease known as Exophthalmic Goitre must not be mistaken for the condition here mentioned. The drawing, which is taken from Mrs. Sutton, a publican's wife in this town, represents the appearance to be noted. Mrs. Sutton has an exceedingly good memory for what she has read. She can repeat almost word for word, she and her husband have

VERBAL MEMORY.

told me, anything she has once read in a newspaper.

I have never met with a marked case of the enlargement known as Number, but it has been found present in calculating boys, such as George Bidder, Zhera Colburn the American, Alexander Gwin, and others. It appears at each of the outermost angles of the eyebrows. Colburn when six years old could answer correctly in twenty seconds how many hours there were in 1811, and a few years later solved more complicated problems. As he grew up his remarkable faculty disappeared, doubtless from excess in its use, coupled with ill-health. Gwin as a boy of eight years of age was, in 1841, employed on the Ordnance Survey of Ireland, and it has been written of him : " He has got by rote the fractional logarithms from one to 1000, which he will repeat in regular rotation or otherwise, as the interrogator may please to put the questions. It is certainly astonishing to think so tender a mind can retain with such tenacity and correctness, seven figures of an answer (according to their different

variations) for 1000 numbers. His rapidity
and correctness in the various calculations
of trigonometrical distances, triangles, &c.,
are amazing beyond anything we have ever
witnessed. He can in less than one minute
make a return in acres, roods, perches, &c.,
of any quantity of land, by giving him the
surveyor's chained distances; while the
greatest arithmetician, with all his knowledge,
will take nearly an hour to do the same, and
not be certain of truth in the end."

The *Lancet* of February 20th, 1892, reports
the following from Paris :—" *Poeta nascitur
non fit.* The feats of Jacques Inaudi at the
Académie des Sciences last Monday week seem
to prove that the above axiom is as applicable
to arithmeticians as to poets. Inaudi is a
native of Piedmont, twenty-four years old,
and of short stature. The size of the head is
rather below the normal standard, the forehead is very lofty and straight, and the facial
angle well developed. That his calculating
powers are of a very high order, and his
memory something quite extraordinary, is
proved by the following experiments per-

formed before the assembled academicians.
Facing the audience, and consequently turning his back to the blackboard, M. Darboux
writes on this latter the following figures:—

4,123,547,238,445,523,831,

and 1,248,126,158,234,128,910,

and, after having called them out, asks Inaudi
to subtract one from the other. Inaudi
repeats the numbers quite correctly, closes
his eyes firmly, and immediately answers
correctly. M. Darboux then puts the following question: 'What number is it whose
square and cube added together equal 3600?'
In less than two seconds Inaudi replies, '15.'
M. Poincarré then gives the following pro-
blem:—'Give the square of 4800, subtract
one and divide by six,' at the same time
M. Bertrand asks: 'On what day of the
week did March 11th, 1822, fall?' Inaudi
replies immediately, 'The 11th of March,
1822, was a Monday, and a person born on
that day would have lived to-day, had he sur-
vived, so many hours, minutes, and seconds.'
(All these figures were found correct.) 'The
result of the calculation proposed by M.

Poincarré is 1960.' These astonishing feats
of rapid calculation greatly surprised the
scientific men present, and the Academy forth-
with appointed a committee, composed of
MM. Darboux, Poincarré, Charcot, Chau-
veau, and Tisserand, whose duty it will be
to report on the mnemotechnic methods employed by this wonder of the nineteenth
century.   It is said that Inaudi can hardly
read or write." *

It will be seen that these extraordinary
calculators have wonderful memories for the
figures which they can so rapidly and correctly multiply, subtract, &c.

The " facial angle" is estimated according
to the amount of projection of the face from
the head.   If the face projects much the angle
is acute, and *vice versâ*.   The facial angle is of
no value in estimating the amount of intellect.

Neither   have   I   seen   very   prominently

---

* Mons. Kleinan, of the firm Messrs. Hachette & Co.,
London and Paris, has very kindly tried to obtain for me
a plaster cast of Inaudi's head, but has failed.   I am,
therefore, unable to give a representation of this calcu-
lator's head.

displayed the next one to Number, namely, Order, but with regard to it, Major Noel told me that he was once travelling in Switzerland, and in conversation with three German students the subject of phrenology was discussed. Finding my friend was learned in the science, the students wanted him to "tell their bumps." He would not do this, but he said he would make one remark, and that was that one of them had evidently the faculty of Order. On his pointing out the possessor of this bump, the other two were in raptures, eagerly bearing testimony to the correctness of Major Noel's statement. They said that their companion was a great nuisance; that they in their travels, for economy's sake, slept in one room, and the first thing he always did was to chalk out his share of the chamber, and neither of the others was allowed to make any use of that portion.

Sciences requiring much study will breed quackery if the practice of them be profitable. Phrenology undoubtedly does. Sir James Crichton-Browne, the well-known alienist, now a Commissioner of Lunacy, aptly shows in a recent letter to me how professional phrenology is not always the archetype, but is sometimes an adumbration, of the science. He says, "I think the phrenology of fifty years ago was worthy of all praise, but the phrenology of to-day is sheer quackery—a mixture of infantine metaphysics and unsound physiology . . . Of course, what I say about the phrenology of to-day refers to its platform manifestations." Some professional phrenologists of to-day deal largely in generalities, entering upon such questions as "May cousins marry?" And instead of giving the salient points of the character before them, are prone to attempt to curry favour with the public by pronouncing too many and too positive opinions on the heads of ordinarily-minded people, concerning whom very little can be said which is complimentary.

If those wishing to study phrenology appreciate the fact that the brain is the reservoir of all thought, that the various sizes and shapes of brains make "all sorts

and conditions of men," that the brain
necessarily is covered (protected) by the
skull, and that this bony skull adapts itself
to the size and shape of its brain, they will
have begun their studies on a sound basis.

Since writing the first edition of this book,
I have seen a letter in a Ramsgate newspaper,
in which an anonymous writer has had the
temerity to put the following : " I have had
excellent opportunities of examining the
human skull, and I fail to see how it is that
small bumps on the outer surface of the
skull can indicate anything of a person's
character, when there is nothing corresponding with the said bumps on the inner side of
the bony structure ; and anybody who has
handled a human skull will know that the
inner side is as smooth as a tea-cup." Little
service this writer's excellent opportunities
of examining the human skull have been to
him. A first year's medical student could
show him how the inner surface of a skull,
though smooth to the touch, is marked with
many depressions, some of which have
corresponding eminences on the outer sur-

face of the bone. If this writer had taken a plaster cast of the inside of the top of a human skull and compared it with the same piece of skull, he could never have written such an incorrect statement.

Professor Sir George M. Humphry, of Cambridge, has written in his " Treatise on the Human Skeleton " :—" We have found that, both in its primitive membranous and in its subsequent ossifying state, the skull is moulded upon the brain and grows in accordance with it. It is subservient to the brain, and there can be no question that the size and general shape of the brain may be estimated with tolerable accuracy by the size and general shape of the skull; and, further, that we may form a pretty correct notion of the relative proportions of the cerebral lobes by observing the proportions of the corresponding parts of the skull. The opponents of phrenology, by denying this, do not in the least advantage their cause in the estimation of thinking persons, because the statement is of a kind at once to commend itself to common sense as being highly probable. . . . The arguments against phrenology—if by phrenology be understood the assigning particular faculties of the mind to particular portions of the brain, and mapping out the skull accordingly—must be of a deeper kind than this to convince anyone who has carefully considered the subject."

Those wishing to possess a thorough knowledge of the science should first learn anatomy, osteology, and physiology. Phrenology, to be studied correctly, requires constant practice in measuring heads, looking at their general shape, and examining them with the hands in order to find out and to appreciate the size of the bumps, especially those which are covered by the hair. But let it be understood that the study should be made discreetly, and time given for perfecting the knowledge ; and, when the lesson is learnt, that common-sense be not forgotten, as it was in the case of Lord Macaulay's fellow-travellers.

It is the unseen and the unknown which disturb so many minds. For instance, the Mahatma belief. Anybody connected with a prison has, at times, to ask why gaping crowds will waste so much time in watching at the gaol gates when practically there is nothing to be seen. And it must be granted that some sciences seem to certain folk to lead to the wonderful. The knowledge of medicine and surgery makes many a man a wonder in the eyes of his fellows. It is so with phrenology. Imagination may be, according to our good Chancellor of the Exchequer, a mental commodity worth encouraging, but let it be mixed with common-sense.

For a long time past I have given up taking measurements of heads, and examining for phrenological bumps. Seeing anybody for the first time, I instinctively look at his head, that I may, as I have before remarked, have an immediate insight into the character; and such an observation takes no more time to make than this paragraph to write, but one has gained, I always feel convinced, a correct judgment of the mental stature of the man whose head one has observed.

In making an estimate of a head, judge first of its size and general shape, and then proceed to note any particular variation. It is not my purpose to give rules for learning the art of phrenology, which should be studied not only by the eyes but also by the hands, so that, were one blindfolded, one's sense of touch could determine the character of the head under examination. I will therefore only briefly relate what is the proper method for measuring heads, and mention some of the general laws to be followed.

The circumference of a head should be taken with a tape or flexible metal measure, placing it over the most prominent parts of the forehead and of the back of the head. In ascertaining the circumference of a head, the thickness of the hair, about a quarter of an inch, must be allowed for.

A very large circumference head-measure for an adult male is $24\frac{1}{2}$ inches ; a moderate one 21 to 22 inches ; a small one 20 inches ; and a head of 13 inches circumference of necessity requires its adult owner to be an idiot. The average sized female head measures less than the average sized male head, accordingly the average weight of a woman's brain is less, being 44 ozs., or 2 lbs. 12 ozs., as compared to 50 ozs., or 3 lbs. 2 ozs., of a man's. The brain of a man is $\frac{1}{40}$th to $\frac{1}{60}$th of the weight of his body, a dog's being about $\frac{1}{120}$th, and a horse's $\frac{1}{750}$th. A German physiologist, Dr. Weisbach, has estimated the cubic contents of a female skull to be to that of a man as 878 is to 1000. Amongst the heaviest known human brains are those of Cuvier, the French comparative anatomist and national educationist, of Abercrombie, the Scotch physician, and of Dupuytreu, the French surgeon. All of these noted men were living at the beginning of this century. Their brains weighed respectively 64 ozs. or 4 lbs., 63 ozs. or 3 lbs. 15 ozs., and 62 ozs. The brain of a new-born infant is from 10 to 12 ozs., increasing so rapidly that by the time the child is seven years old it weighs 40 ozs. The brain of a full-grown gorilla happily, let it be noted, is never more than about 15 ozs. The brain of an idiot adult is about a third that of a sane man's, ranging from 1 lb. (16 ozs.) to 1 lb. 8 ozs.

Elephants and whales have larger brains than man, the former's weighing 10 lbs., the latter's 6 lbs. An Indian elephant weighs four tons,* and therefore its brain is $\frac{1}{900}$th of the weight of its body ; a fin whale weighs fifty tons,* and therefore its brain is $\frac{1}{17300}$th.

With regard to the relation between the brains of men and animals, Gall has written that the qualities and faculties which are common to man and animals have, roughly speaking, their seat in the inferior portions of the brain ; but that those which man exclusively enjoys, and which form the barrier by which he is separated from the brute, have their seat in those parts which are for the great part wanting in animals; namely, the anterior and superior portions of the brain.

An easy method of finding out the circumference of a man's head, if he be a friend and supposing that we know the size of our own head (and this should be a phrenologist's first study), is to put on his hat. See what Monsieur Léon, the enterprising hatter in

* These weights are according to the high authority of Dr. Günther, of the British Museum.

F

Paris, says in his pamphlet, "Têtes et Chapeaux" (1891) :—" Par l'étude des chapeaux, je le disais dans un précédent chapitre, je suis arrivé insensiblement à étudier les différentes conformations des têtes et, depuis longtemps déjà, j'ai constaté que la forme des crânes vraie selon les races, les positions sociales et surtout selon les degrés de l'intelligence. Ce qui frappa d'abord en faisant mes premières observations. . . . Personne ne conteste aujourd'hui que le cerveau est l'instrument matériel de la pensée ; de même que le gros biceps indiquent des bras puissants, une tête forte indique évidemment de grandes pensées bonnes ou mauvaises, de grandes qualités on de grands défauts.   Quelle belle chose que la science ! "

The *Pall Mall Gazette* last year, in a notice of M. Leon's pamphlet, wrote the following :— " . . . . We find that we gave a representation *tam cari capitis* a year or two ago, among several others, from the portfolio of Mr. Henry Heath. But the head of the Prince of Wales brings us to the puzzle. It is the only diagram of which we have

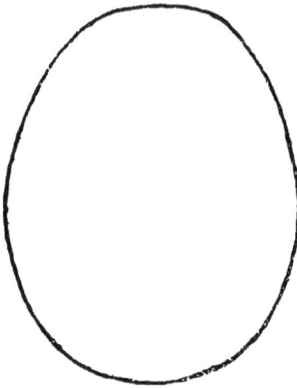

PRINCE OF WALES.   PRINCE OF WALES.

From Mr. Heath's pamphlet.   From M. Leon's pamphlet.

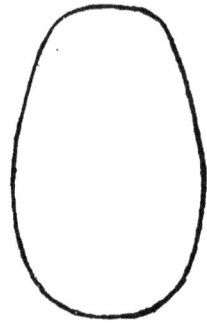

(Taken from the *Pall Mall Gazette*, September 22nd, 1891.)

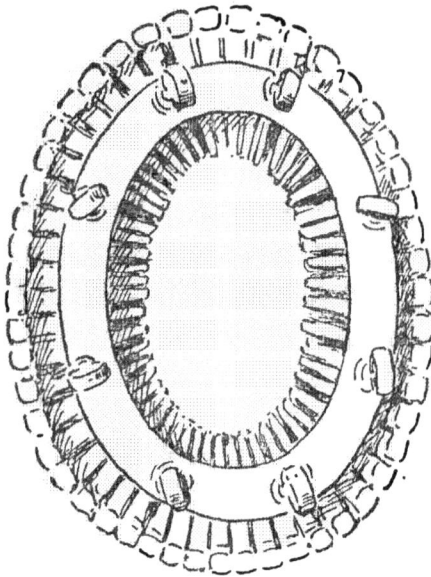

HATTER'S " BROW."

2 F

versions from both the French and the English hatter, and—well, they differ considerably. Possibly one was taken at a more hirsute period of life . . . but this is delicate ground, and not even this surely would account for such a huge divergence of shape. Why, Mr. Heath's Prince couldn't walk away with M. Leon's Prince's hat from the club. And we must say that some of the Frenchman's other figures rather puzzle us, especially the very ' long-headed ' American type, and the fiddle-shape which M. Leon attributes to his countrymen and to Baron Rothschild. But who shall confute the *conformateur ?* And who shall decide where hatters disagree ? "

The *Pall Mall's* puzzle is explained as follows :—Hatters use an instrument called " Brow " (represented in the drawing on the previous page), which can be made to fit any sized hat by means of screws. The outside of this instrument is the actual shape and measurement of a head, and the inside is the key to this shape. But the inside shape of the " Brow " is not a reduction of the shape of the head in due proportion, for the same deduction is made all round, in length and width, and therefore the proportion is lost. M. Leon's representations of heads are sketched from the inside shapes (" long-headed" and "fiddle-shaped ") of his " Brow," whereas Mr. Heath's are from the outside measurements of his instrument.

Hatter's measurement is the medium of the length and breadth inside brim measurements of a hat combined. Thus a hat is 8 inches long and 7 inches broad. These two measurements make together 15 inches, and the half of that total will be $7\frac{1}{2}$, which is $7\frac{1}{2}$ inches diameter or hatter's measurement. The average measurement of a new-born infant has been found to be 5 inches ; of a one-year-old child, $5\frac{5}{8}$ inches ; of a seven years' old, $6\frac{1}{2}$ inches ; of a twelve years' old child, $6\frac{3}{4}$ inches.* Hatter's measurements are as follows :—

* These measurements, taken from Professor Humphry's previously mentioned work, Messrs. Swears and Wells, of Regent Street, have assured me are, according to their experience, correct.

Hatter's measurement :— $5\frac{7}{8}$ 6 $6\frac{1}{8}$ $6\frac{1}{4}$ $6\frac{3}{8}$ $6\frac{1}{2}$ $6\frac{5}{8}$ $6\frac{3}{4}$
Circumference of head :—$18\frac{1}{2}$ $18\frac{7}{8}$ $19\frac{1}{4}$ $19\frac{5}{8}$ 20 $20\frac{1}{2}$ $20\frac{7}{8}$ $21\frac{1}{4}$
Hatter's measurement :— $6\frac{7}{8}$ 7 $7\frac{1}{8}$ $7\frac{1}{4}$ $7\frac{3}{8}$ $7\frac{1}{2}$ $7\frac{5}{8}$ $7\frac{3}{4}$
Circumference of head :—$21\frac{5}{8}$ 22 $22\frac{3}{8}$ $22\frac{3}{4}$ $23\frac{1}{4}$ $23\frac{5}{8}$ 24 $24\frac{3}{8}$

Messrs. Lincoln and Bennett, who have afforded me much generous assistance, have verified the above adult measurements. They tell me that the size for male adults mostly in demand is $6\frac{7}{8}$; that the largest and smallest hats ordinarily required amongst their customers are respectively $7\frac{3}{4}$ and $6\frac{1}{2}$. They have made one hat of $7\frac{7}{8}$ or $24\frac{6}{8}$ inches circumference of head, and one of $6\frac{3}{8}$. This latter was for a colonel in Her Majesty's army, and therefore we may presume that, though the size of this gentleman's hat was so small, his head must have been a remarkably well-formed one.

Messrs. Lincoln and Bennett have also kindly shown me the models of some extraordinary sized heads. General Tom Thumb's of $5\frac{3}{4}$, or $18\frac{3}{8}$ inches circumference; General Mite's of $5\frac{1}{8}$, or $16\frac{3}{8}$ inches; and one of a gentleman whose head slowly increased in size during adult life from $7\frac{3}{4}$ to $8\frac{1}{2}$ or 27 inches circumference. This increase was due to thickening of the skull bones, a disease known by the name of Osteo Deformans.

That I might be able to compare these measurements of the West End with the sizes of hats used by the "coster" class I have applied to Mr. T. Clark, of the New Cut, Lambeth, and to Mr. E. Hillier, of Mile End Road, and they both very kindly have given me full information. Mr. Clark writes that his sizes run from $6\frac{3}{8}$ to $7\frac{1}{8}$, $6\frac{5}{8}$ being the size mostly used; that it is very seldom that he sells any men's hats larger than $7\frac{1}{8}$, or smaller than $6\frac{3}{8}$. Mr. Hillier finds his sizes run from $6\frac{1}{4}$ to $7\frac{3}{8}$ for men's hats, the largest sale being for $6\frac{5}{8}$ and $6\frac{3}{4}$. Mr. Hillier makes the curious statement that, with an average sale of 3000 hats per week, he finds that the sizes of hats required at the present time are less than they were ten years ago.

It has been stated by Deeming's solicitor in Australia (April, 1892) that the head of this commonly-believed family and general murderer,* and also thief, only measures $6\frac{1}{4}$

* Found guilty, and hung May 23rd, 1892.

inches ; and that, if Deeming is guilty of the crimes ascribed to him, he must be held irresponsible, because a man with so small a head cannot be held accountable for his actions, although such actions have tended to his own benefit.

To many people $6\frac{1}{4}$ inches measurement is bewildering. The explanation must be that $6\frac{1}{4}$ is the measurement of Deeming's hat, such measurement giving $19\frac{5}{8}$ circumference of head. Judging from the representations of Deeming in the illustrated papers, I do not believe that this measurement given by the astute lawyer is correct; and if Deeming is the murderer and thief he is represented to be, he would certainly, I should say, require a head of larger circumference than $19\frac{5}{8}$ to have planned the murders and thefts, all of which seem to have been executed with much intelligence and constructive ability. It is not the size of a head which makes a murderer and a thief, but it is peculiarities of shape which produce such tendencies, namely Destructiveness and Acquisitiveness.

The circumference of a head and hatter's

measurement, it must be remembered, are not absolute guides to the size of a head, for they do not give any idea of the height of the head. Hatter's measurement in many cases gives less circumference than the tape of the phrenologist, for the latter takes the largest measurement he can, probably low down on the back of the head and immediately above the eyebrows.

Calipers are used for measuring the length of a head, the width across the brows, and above the ears ; and this instrument is necessary for reckoning the distances from the opening of an ear to the forehead, from the ear to the top of the head, and from the ear to the back of the head.

At the time of noting the size of a head we should see whether the fore-half is equal to its back-half, the fore-half being thought by phrenologists to contain the intellectual portion of the brain, the back-half having more relation to the energy of the man. The following drawings represent two men with about equal sized heads. If there is any difference between them it is that the

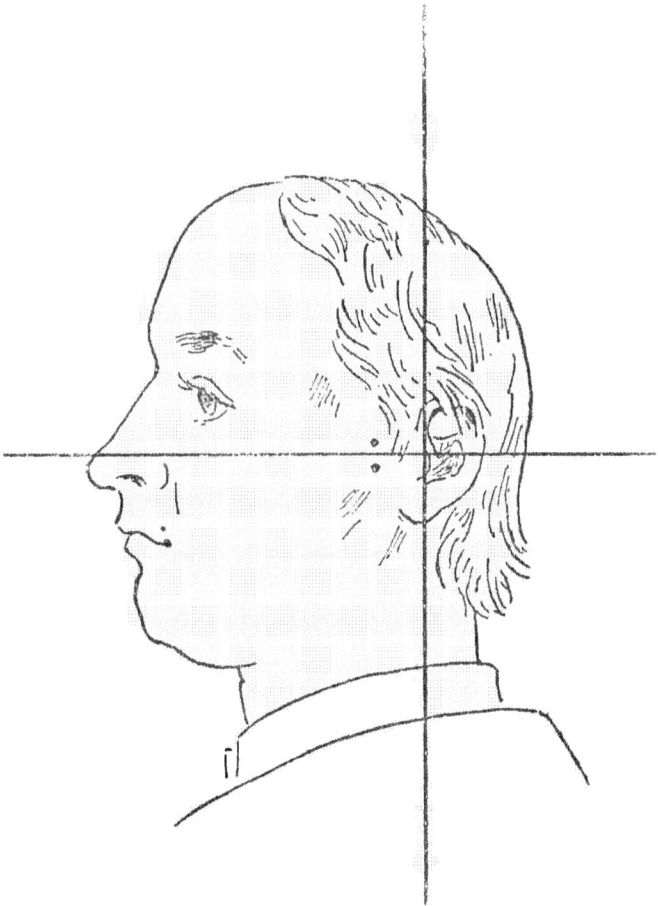

"FORE-HALF" LARGE.

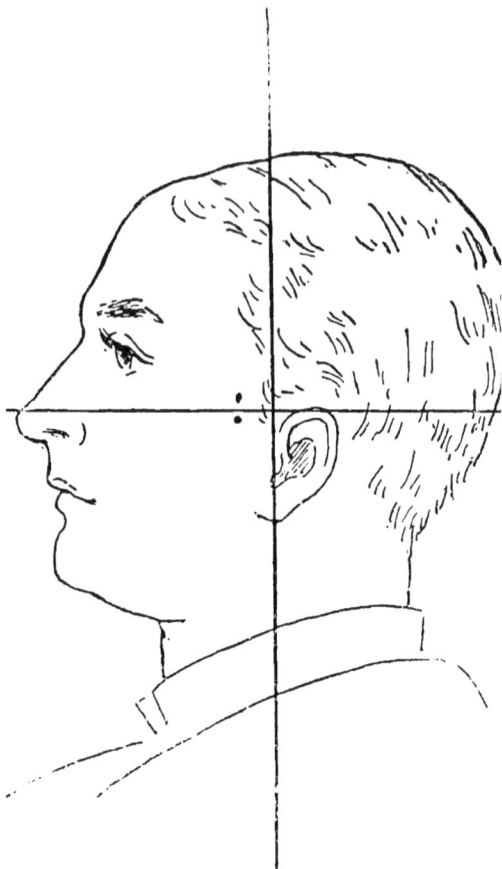

' BACK-HALF " LARGE.

head of the second one is the larger, but hardly the most casual observer would judge that this one, marked " back-half large," had in any degree the same amount of intellect. It fairly represents a man of the world, whereas the other is that of a man fitted for the quiet and refined research of a library.

The horizontal and vertical lines mark the divisions which the eye of the phrenologist at once maps out. The horizontal line is taken through two spots which are on the most prominent part of the cheek-bone, the Zygomatic process of the Temporal bone, at its junction with the Malar bone. This point very nearly coincides with the lowest part of the front lobe of the three lobes of the brain, and therefore it is a fair standard level to take. The vertical line, drawn so that it runs down in front of the ear, is in an imaginary position with regard to any division of the brain, but it separates the head into the two portions which we may recognize as the intellectual and the energetic.

Old English writers on phrenology divided

the mental faculties into two Orders, and
these again into Genera. They called the
two Orders " Affective " and " Intellectual,"
dividing the former into " Propensities " and
" Sentiments," the latter into " Perceptive
Faculties " and " Reflective Faculties."
They marked plaster casts of heads into so
many divisions, giving the spaces such titles
as Destructiveness, Constructiveness, &c.
Doubtless they did not intend the lines of these
divisions to be arbitrary, or the titles they
gave the divisions to be other in their abrupt-
ness than useful terms. As the late Major
Noel has pointed out, Dr. Gall is not an-
swerable for their doing so. " He merely
marked little circles on skulls indicating the
parts he had observed to be prominent in
unusual instances of predominant dispositions, talents, &c."

And again, " Dr. Gall designated all the
special faculties, the seats of which in the
brain he believed he had discovered, 'instincts'
or 'inner senses.' " He named the parts
which are now known as Destructiveness
as " Instinct Carnassier, penchant au meutre,"

and Constructiveness as " Sens de meca-
nique, sens de construction." " Phrenologists
generally," Major Noel has written, "moreover commit the error of seeming to personify
faculties, by saying ' Destructiveness does
this,' ' Love of Approbation (Gall's vanité
ambition, amour de la gloire) does that,'
&c., thus conveying the impression of want of
co-relation or combined activity in the faculties of the mind."

Gall found and named twenty-seven faculties. Later phrenologists, notably Spurzheim, have added ten more.

They are as follows:—

Amativeness.	Benevolence.
Philoprogenitiveness.	Veneration.
Concentrativeness.	Firmness.
Inhabitiveness.	Conscientiousness.
Adhesiveness.	Hope.
Combativeness.	Wonder.
Destructiveness.	Ideality.
Alimentiveness.	Wit.
Secretiveness.	Imitation.
Acquisitiveness.	Individuality.
Constructiveness.	Form.
Self-Esteem.	Size.
Love of approbation.	Weight.
Cautiousness.	Colouring.

G

Locality.	Tune.
Number.	Language.
Order.	Comparison.
Eventuality.	Causality.
Time.	

Those wishing to see the position of these faculties, as marked out by Dr. Gall and others, should purchase a phrenological bust of the head; at the same time being careful to ascertain that it is correctly marked.

The lines in the drawings enable one to gain an idea of the height and length of the brain. The width has to be estimated by a front view of the head. It may be remarked that to estimate character from photographs, one taken full-face and another from a side view of the head should be used. But photographs often give a deceptive idea of the elevation of a head, making it appear loftier than it is.

After noticing the general size of a head, one observes the formation of the top of the head. If the crown is well raised, as in the frontispiece, uprightness of character is signified. If the crown is flat, or depressed in the centre as seen in the drawing on page 34, the reverse, as stated before, may be expected.

Horses and dogs which have full foreheads are found to be much better-tempered than those with sunken foreheads.

A front view of a head gives the height of the forehead, the breadth of the brow, and the fulness or flatness of the sides of the head. Height of the forehead points to reflective qualities; breadth of brow to perceptive qualities; and fulness of the sides of the forehead to idealistic (see drawing), musical, poetical, and other artistic qualities. Also to Wit (Gall's esprit caustique; esprit de saillie), Constructiveness* or mechanical power, &c. Breadth between the eyes, it is noticed, is largely present with artists, giving them a full appreciation of Form

---

* The principal glass-workers at Salviati's forge at Venice in London (1892) were said to belong to one family. And also it was stated that this family had for 400 years held pre-eminence in the manufacture of glass vases, &c. It was very interesting to note how large an amount of Constructiveness was present in all of their heads.

(Gall's Mémoire des personnes; sens des personnes), and Size. These two faculties are the inner ones of a set of six which phrenologists place along the upper eyebrow. The remainder from the nose outwards are Weight or Resistance, Colour (Gall's Sens des rapports des coleurs ; talent de la peinture), Number (Gall's Sens des rapports des nombres), and Order. Between the two sets above the root of the nose come the three, Individuality, Eventuality (taken as one by Gall, mémoire des choses; mémoire des faits; sens des choses; éducabilité; perfectibilité; but made two by Spurzheim), and Locality (Gall's Sens des localités, sens des rapports de l'éspace). It is in this portion of the forehead that air cells in connection with the nostrils are present, and which are deceptive to the student of " bumpology."

It is to be regretted that liars have not a bump situated in the centre of the forehead, and better still would it be if this bump would appear congested whenever its owner was allowing himself, or herself, to say what was not true. Such a phrenological beacon

IDEALITY.

(Mr. Bernard Collier, late Master of the Sidney Cooper
School of Art, Canterbury.)

would save our judges much time, and free them from much anxiety.

The head shown in the frontispiece is a specimen of a remarkably well-shaped head. It is from a drawing of the late Mr. Cullen Bryant, of New York.

Kind people are often called "good-hearted." And, again, it is a common expression, "how much he will take that to heart." Whether many believe that any feelings actually arise in the substance of the heart, I would not say; but, of course, all such feelings have their origin in the brain. Therefore, the Irishman in *Punch* went half-way towards the truth when, asked by his parson how it was he could be alive if shot in the region of the body he described, he answered, "Sure, yer rivirence, my heart was in my mouth." Phrenology places the higher feelings in the upper portions of the two hemispheres, allotting Benevolence (Gall's Bonté; bienveillance; douceur; sensibilité; sens morale; conscience), Veneration (Gall's Sentiment religieux; Dieu et la Religion), Conscientiousness (Spurzheim's), and Hope (Spurzheim's) to the vault of the head.

I know that many, very many, I may say, pooh-pooh the idea that the science called phrenology is of any value, but I have never met a single person who has studied the subject fully who would wish to deny the correctness of its teaching.

The many instances of phrenological bumps seen on the heads of children with precocious talents, and on the heads of men and women of striking character, and the association of these bumps with the owner's separate peculiarities, unmistakably point to the truthfulness of the science.

A large head does not necessarily, as I have before premised, command a high order of intellect, but it may, on the other hand, mean intellect without energy, or energy without intellect. Or, again, its owner may be clever without possessing conscientious-ness or benevolence. Therefore some of us may consider that it is better under certain circumstances to possess a small, well-formed head than a large one. .

That a large, well-formed head, in making the man, is witness to the truth of phrenology, I need but instance the case of the greatest physician in England, Sir William Jenner. We all know him well by repute as the much-trusted adviser of Her Gracious Majesty the Queen, and as one beloved by his own profession.

Then, again, in the case of Prince Bismarck—that, till lately, stupendous power in Germany and Europe. There is no need to speak of his qualities, or to differentiate between his head and that of Sir William Jenner. Of both these public men a phrenologist, without knowing them, would say that whatever they did would be done honestly, and, if they were statesmen, that their aim would be that their work should prove to be for their country's good. Apart from phrenology, I would remark that it has been said that Prince Bismarck is rough and overbearing, and a man of no feeling except for himself. Those who are not acquainted with him, but who have read the late John Lothrop Motley's corre-

spondence, will remember the style of many
of Prince Bismarck's letters to his bosom-
friend, especially the one commencing,
" Jack, dear, why the devil don't you write
to me ? " and will draw their own con-
clusions regarding such a man's friendship.
Even the short sentence I have quoted seems
to speak volumes.

Some time ago I asked at Messrs. Lincoln
and Bennett's who, amongst their customers,
took the largest-sized hat. I was told that
Mr. Fawcett, the Postmaster-General, did,
or rather the second largest size of any
they supplied. Now to fill the office of
Postmaster-General would require, under
ordinary circumstances, a clever man, but
for the position to have been filled and the
work to have been carried out successfully
by a blind gentleman, must have required
a very large brain.

With regard to the shape of the head
conveying an idea of character, I would
mention that in the *Graphic* or in the
Illustrated London News, three or four years
ago, the portrait of Queen Natalie of Servia

was given. I judged at once by the shape of this lady's head that she was possessed of great energy, but that she would in all likelihood be ill-advised in what she did, and that her persistent action against the Servian Government after her husband's (King Milan's) abdication would not be for her country's good. I knew then, and know now, but little of the circumstances of the Servian disturbance; at the same time, I believe that my estimate of this Queen's character has been borne out by what has since happened.

The size of the skull belonging to the skeleton which was found in the crypt of Canterbury Cathedral in January, 1888, and which was supposed by many to be that of Thomas à Becket, was to me one of the strong proofs that the bones, which I put together, were those of the great archbishop. The bones of the head, when fitted on a mould of modeller's clay, formed an almost perfect skull. This skull was far above the ordinary size; in fact, I should say its measurements were those we should give to a large head—that is, a skull with all the integuments on. The circumference measurement with the tape, $22\frac{3}{4}$ inches, would certainly not on a covered skull (skin, &c.) have been less than another inch. The width of the brow was in like proportion, measuring from the external angles of each orbit with the tape $5\frac{1}{2}$ inches, with the calipers 5 inches.

I am quite aware that the question of whose bones they could have been can never, for want of documentary evidence, be proved or disproved. Still there could be no doubt that the skull belonged to a man of immense mental power and energy, and therefore something should have been known of his re-burial* in a stone coffin, in the most sacred part of the old cathedral.

---

* This re-burial, which it undoubtedly was, could not have taken place, according to Canon Scott Robertson in Vol. xiii. of *Archæologia Cantiana*, since 1546, eight years after the destruction of Becket's shrine by Henry the Eighth, for the portion of crypt in which the bones were found was from 1546 to 1866 used as a private cellar by the Senior Canon. It may be further remarked that the bones, which beyond doubt were ancient, belonged to a man of about Becket's stature, who was very

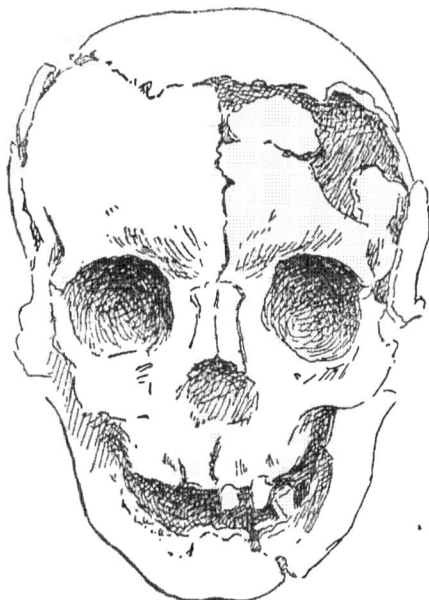

FRONT VIEW OF SKULL, SUPPOSED BY MANY TO BE THOMAS
À BECKET'S, SHOWING GREAT WIDTH OF BROW.

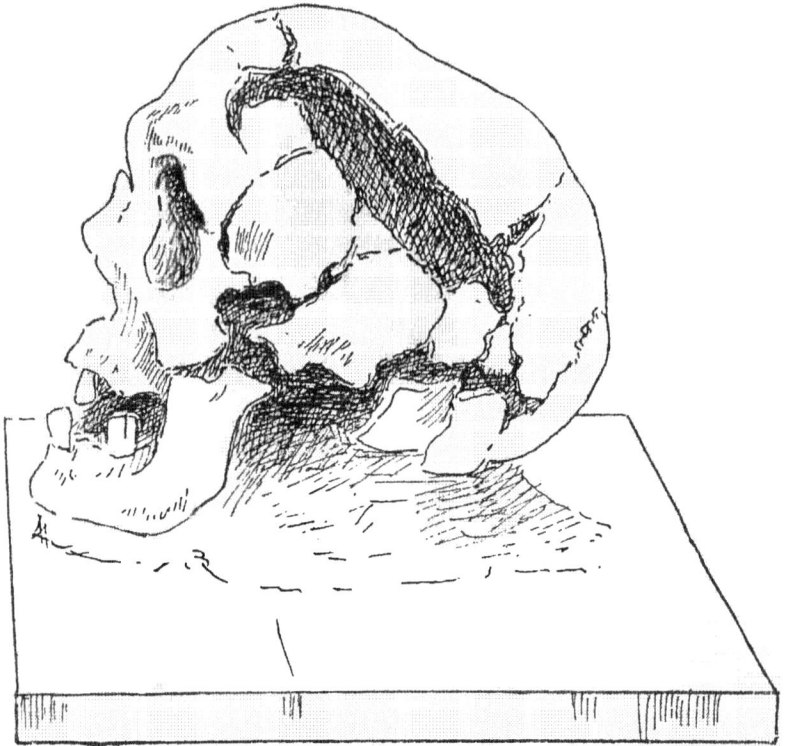

SIDE VIEW OF SAME SKULL, SHOWING DEPRESSION OF CENTRE OF THE CROWN.

The configuration of this skull showed depression of the centre of the crown portion. Whether the character of such a skull agrees with that known of Thomas à Becket I leave to others more acquainted with ecclesiastical history to determine. Mr. Arthur G. Hill, Fellow of the Society of Antiquaries, has written in the *Newbery House Magazine* of July, 1890, " History does not reveal in him any qualities which especially go to form the Christian Saint."

The late Major Noel told me that when he was in the Service he used, as far as circumstances would permit, to choose his sergeants by the shape of their heads. My present servants, man and wife, I took almost entirely by the character their heads gave them, only knowing that the man was the brother of a friend's servant. I well remember their astonishment when

tall, and about his age, fifty-two years. The side view of the skull, it will be noted, shows an aperture. It is the straightness of the bone for five to six inches, forming the upper border of this aperture, which has caused discussion as to whether it might not be due to a sword-cut.

H

I accepted their services without asking questions, and without reading the written characters. They have now been with me for more than five years, and they have proved themselves to be, I am glad to say, what I phrenologically judged them to be.

Of course, heads and faces go together, but I would say that the head forms the face; and, further, that a face may pass muster when a head may not bear evidence of good character.

In concluding, I would ask that phrenology may be acknowledged to be an honest science, and that it may be thought useful in more ways than one. Take, for instance, the important question of the management of children. Through understanding phrenology we may see more clearly in what direction we should try to guide them. Schoolmasters would find the knowledge particularly useful, for it gives a rapid and sure insight into the peculiarities and the mental powers of a child.

Phrenology certainly does not tend to materialism. Gall, writing on the arrange-

ment of the faculties as shown by phrenology,
says : " We discover there the hand of God,
Whom we cannot cease to adore with the
more astonishment, in proportion as His
works are more displayed before our eyes "
(translated by Dr. Macuish).

REVIEWS OF FIRST EDITION.

"A plea for the truth of phrenology as a science. The author relates cases within his own experience in which the configuration of the head has proved an index of character."—*Morning Post.*

"Oddly enough, ' Firmness' (very like Prince Bismarck) is merely our old friend of the third-class ticket, with the dome of his brain raised a trifle. Depress Prince Bismarck's head, and he swindles railway ticket-collectors. Raise it, and he takes Alsace and Lorraine. Yet Phrenology does not tend to 'materialism,' says Mr. Thornton. Of course he seems to be mistaken. Our characters follow our bumps, which we made not, neither can mend, not our bumps our characters."—*Daily News.*

"The sceptical and credulous may alike find interest in this little book—the recollections of a phrenologist of twelve years' standing. . . . It is precisely the extravagance which brings it ofttimes into ridicule now, and Mr. Thornton has wisely recognized this in writing his little book, which is not only very readable, but contains nothing that is not eminently reasonable."—*Daily Graphic.*

"In a pleasing and chatty style, the author, while telling some interesting recollections of his phrenological experiences, enables the reader to obtain a practical knowledge of phrenology. The book is far superior to most of the works that are issued on this subject."—*Manchester Courier.*

"Mr. Pugin Thornton admits that very many people pooh-pooh the idea that the science called phrenology is of any value, but he says he has never met a single person who has studied the subject fully who would wish to deny the correctness of its teaching. Not having studied the subject fully ourselves, we express no opinion either way; there may be something in it or there may not. We prefer to have an 'open mind' on the subject, as Mr. Gladstone has on a variety of subjects. We can certainly recommend Mr. Thornton's little treatise to all who have a weakness for phrenology."—*Kentish Observer.*

"It will be of special interest to readers who give attention to phrenology, and some portions will be entertaining to an even wider circle. The pages are occasionally enlivened by some good anecdotes, and the illustrations by Ellen Welby, showing the different shapes of the heads of well-known people, give the book pictorial value."—*Bristol Observer.*

". . . . . and published by Messrs. Sampson Low at the moderate price of 1s. The little work abounds with some interesting reminiscences and phrenological recollections. The different types of character are illustrated with sketches by Miss Ellen Welby. . . . The book, which is altogether of anecdotal character, will serve to pleasantly pass a spare hour."—*Kentish Gazette.*

"Phrenology must be a wonderful science. According to Mr. Pugin Thornton, whose book, 'Heads, and what They Tell

Us,' has met with no little success, a clever phrenologist does not need to feel the bumps of his subject, but can tell at a glance whether the person before him be good or bad tempered, a murderer, a thief, or merely travelling in a first-class carriage with a third-class ticket; all, of course, provided the subject be sufficiently bald-headed for the purpose. . . . The Eminent intends shortly to publish a book written by himself, entitled, 'Noses, and what They Tell us.' A. Sloper's nose tells us a good deal, and a very considerable amount is certainly not to his credit."—*Ally Sloper.*

"This book is a series of phrenological recollections extending over a period of some years. The work contains some excellent information, and the plates ably illustrate the narratives. We are sorry that Mr. Thornton has not written a longer and more comprehensive work, for he makes all his points very clear."—*Key.*

"This is an amusing little book, with some clever pictures by Miss Ellen Welby, but we cannot accept the author's claims for phrenology. He says there is an intimate relation between it and the functions of the brain, a very hazy statement, that, as far as we understand, has no foundation in fact. Nor is there any connection 'between phrenological bumps and the convolutions of the brain;' but the direct contrary has been proved again and again. The general shape of a head may tell us something, but that is all. There are many anecdotes, all tending to the glorification of phrenology."—*Court Circular.*

"This booklet has just been issued in a popular style, and it would be surprising if it did not sell well, not for its scientific pretensions, for it has none, but because it will catch the popular eye. Its salient points are certainly to be found in its readable type, which is large and clear, while the matter is entertaining, though at times open to question. The cuts seem to have been carefully done ; but unfortunately they do not in every case represent what they are supposed to. For instance, on page 16, a cut represents a head that is lacking in veneration, while the organ of consciousness is described. The illustration for large language would puzzle the novice to see any difference between large and small language. Again, on page 49, the forehead taken from a drawing of the late Mr. Cullen Bryant, of New York, is a very poor representation of that remarkable man."—*Phrenological Magazine.**

"Phrenology is attracting so much attention in Ramsgate, and even in our own columns, that we are pleased to have before us this intelligently-written work on the subject. The author does not write exhaustively on the subject, but he touches on it with sufficient gracefulness to make it fascinating."—*Kent Argus.*

"An interesting little volume, written with the evident intention of bringing more clearly before the eyes of the public the theory of Phrenology, has emanated from the pen of Mr. W. P. Thornton. . . . The fault of most writers upon the subject of Phrenology has been their exaggeration of its importance, and in their enthusiasm many have gone so far as to avow that a bump denoting character can be found in every quarter of an inch of the human head. Mr. Thornton wisely refrains from adopting so far-reaching a theory, but he brings strong evidence to prove that the shape of the cranium reflects

* "Unfortunately," too, the *Phrenological Magazine* has not represented, in every case, the facts as they should be. It makes the drawing of Mr. Cullen Bryant appear in the first edition on page 49, whereas "Fore-half large" occupies that position. Mr. Bryant's portrait is both in the first and in this edition the frontispiece. I hardly think—at least, I fain would not believe—that there is any comparison between the drawings of Mr. Bryant and "Fore-half large ;" not even, according to history, that "having paid your money you takes your choice." I fully believe that the drawing of the late Mr. Bryant, of New York, is a good representation of that remarkable man.—W. P. T.

the virtues and vices of men, women, and children. . . . In this light and lucid style the writer engrosses the attention of his reader, and the thought that flashes through the mind of the latter when he closes the book is a resolve to study the science more carefully, for, as Mr. Thornton says, if Phreno-logy is sound, it will be useful in every sphere of life, but more especially in the management of children."—*Ashford News.*

" This is a short treatise of the bumpy science by Mr. W. Pugin Thornton, of which let it suffice to say that it thoroughly exhausts the subject. It is bound in cloth boards, printed on good paper in easily-read type, and is well illustrated."— *Dover Express.*

St. Dunstan's House, Fetter Lane,
London, E.C.   *August*, 1895.

Select List of Books in all Departments of Literature

PUBLISHED BY

Sampson Low, Marston & Company, Ld.

AARON, Dr. E. M., *The Butterfly Hunters in the Caribbees*, 7s. 6d.

ABBEY, C. J., *Religious Thought in Old English Verse*, 5s.

—— and PARSONS, *Quiet Life*, from drawings; motive by Austin Dobson, 31s. 6d.

ABERDEEN, Earl of. See Prime Ministers.

ABNEY, Capt., *Colour Vision*, 12s. 6d.

—— *Instruction in Photography*, 3s. 6d.

—— *Instantaneous Photography*, 1s.

—— *Negative Making*, 1s.

—— *Photography with Emulsions*, 3s.

—— *Platinotype Printing*, 2s. 6d.

—— *Thebes*, 63s.

—— and H. P. ROBINSON, *Art of Silver Printing*, 2s. 6d.

—— and CUNNINGHAM, *Pioneers of the Alps*, new ed. 21s.

About Some Fellows, by "an Eton boy," 2s. 6d. ; new edit. 1s.

ADAM, G. M., *An Algonquin Maiden*, 5s.

—— *Sir J. A. Macdonald's Life*, 16s.

ADAMS, Charles K., *Historical Literature*, 12s. 6d.

AINSLIE, P., *Priceless Orchid*, new ed., 3s. 6d. and 2s. 6d.

AITKEN, R. *Memorials of Burns*, 5s.

ALBERT, Prince. See Bay. S.

ALCOTT, L. M., *Jo's Boys*, 5s.

—— *Comic Tragedies*, 5s.

—— *Life, Letters and Journals*, by Ednah D. Cheney, 6s. ; 3s. 6d. See also " Low's Standard Series for Girls " and Rose Library.

ALDEN, W. L. See Low's Standard Series of Girls' Books.

ALFORD, Lady Marian, *Needlework as Art*, 21s.; l. p. 84s.

ALGER, J. G., *Englishmen in the French Revolution*, 7s. 6d.

—— *Glimpses of the French Revolution*, 6s.

Amateur Angler in Dove Dale, by E. M., 1s. 6d., 1s.

American Catalogue of Books, 1886-94, each 15s. and 18s.

AMICIS, E. de, *Heart*, 3s. 6d.

AMPHLETT, F. H., *Lower and Mid Thames*, 1s.

ANDERSEN, H.C., *Fairy Tales*, illust. by Scandinavian artists, 6s.

ANDERSON, W., *Pictorial Arts of Japan*, 4 parts, 168s.

Angler's strange Experiences, by Cotswold Isys, new edit., 3s. 6d.

BLACK, WILLIAM. See Low's Standard Novels.

—— R., *Death no Bane*, 5s.

—— *History of Horse Racing in France*, 14s.

BLACKBURN, C. F., *Catalogue Titles, Index Entries, &c.* 14s.

——*Rambles in Books*, cr. 8vo. 5s.; edit. de luxe, 15s.

—— H., *Art in the Mountains*, new edit. 5s.

—— *Artistic Travel*, 7s. 6d.

—— *Breton Folk*, n. e., 10s. 6d.

BLACKMORE, R. D., *Georgics of Virgil*, 4s. 6d.; cheap edit. 1s. See also Low's Standard Novels.

BLAIKIE, *How to get Strong*, new edit. 5s.

—— *Sound Bodies for our Boys and Girls*, 2s. 6d.

Boas, Textbook of Zoology. 2 vols.

Bobby, a Story, by Vesper, 1s.

BOCK, *Temples & Elephants*, 21s.

Bonaparte, Decline and fall of, by Wolseley, 3s. 6d.

BONWICK, JAMES, *Colonial Days*, 2s. 6d.

—— *Colonies*, 1s. each; 1 vol. 5s.

—— *Daily Life of the Tasmanians*, 12s. 6d.

—— *First Twenty Years of Australia*, 5s.

—— *Irish Druids*, 6s.

—— *Last of the Tasmanians*, 16s.

—— *Port Philip*, 21s.

—— *Romance of Wool Trade*, 6s.

—— *Lost Tasmanian Race*, 4s.

BOSANQUET, C., *Jehoshaphat*, 1s.

——*Lenten Meditations*, Ser. I. 1s. 6d.; II. 2s.

—— *Tender Grass for Lambs*, 2s. 6d.

BOULTON, *N. W. Rebellions*, Canadian life, 9s.

BOURKE, *On the Border with Crook*, illust., roy. 8vo, 21s.

—— *Snake Dance of Arizona*, with coloured plates, 21s.

BOUSSENARD. See Low's Standard Books.

BOWEN, F., *Modern Philosophy*, new ed. 16s.

BOWER, G. S., and WEBB, *Law of Electric Lighting*, 12s. 6d.

BOWNE, B. P., *Metaphysics*, 12s. 6d.

BOYESEN, H. H., *Against Heavy Odds*, 5s.; also 3s. 6d.

—— *History of Norway*, 7s. 6d.

—— *Modern Vikings*, 3s. 6d.

Boys, vols. I., II., 7s. 6d. each.

BRACE, C. L., *Life*, 8s. 6d.

BRADSHAW, *New Zealand as it is*, 12s. 6d.

—— *New Zealand of To-day*, 14s.

BRANNT, *Fats and Oils*, 42s.

—— *Scourer and Dyer*, 10s. 6d.

—— *Soap and Candles*, 35s.

—— *Vinegar, Acetates*, 25s.

—— *Distillation of Alcohol*, 12s. 6d.

—— *Metal Worker's Receipts*, 12s. 6d.

—— *Metallic Alloys*, 12s. 6d.

—— *Petroleum*, 35s.

—— and WAHL, *Techno-Chemical Receipt Book*, 10s. 6d.

BRETON, JULES, *Life of an Artist*, an autobiography, 7s. 6d.

BRETT, EDWIN J., *Ancient Arms and Armour*, 105s. nett.

BRIGHT, JOHN, *Letters of*, 5s.

BRINE, ADMIRAL L., *Travels*, 21s.

BRISSE, *Menus and Recipes*, French & English, new ed. 3s. 6d.

Britons in Brittany, 2s. 6d.

BROOKS, G., *Industry and Property*, 3s. 6d.
—— Noah, *Boy Settlers*, 6s. ; new ed., 3s. 6d.
—— *Statesmen*, 8s. 6d.
BROWN, A. J., *Rejected of Men*, and other poems, 3s. 6d.
—— A. S. *Madeira and Canary Islands for Invalids*, n. ed. 2s. 6d.
—— *South Africa*, 2s. 6d.
—— Robert. See Low's Standard Novels.
BROWNE, Lennox, and BEHNKE, *Voice, Song, & Speech*, 15s. ; new edit. 5s.
—— *The Child's Voice*, 3s. 6d.
—— *Voice Use*, 3s. 6d.
BRYCE, G., *Manitoba*, 7s. 6d.
—— *Short History of the Canadian People*, 7s. 6d.
BULKELEY, Owen T., *Lesser Antilles*, 2s. 6d.
BUNYAN. See Low's Standard Series.
BURDETT-COUTTS, *Brookfield Stud*, 5s.
—— Baroness, *Woman's Mission*, Congress papers, 10s. 6d.
BURNABY, Evelyn, *Ride from Land's End to John o' Groats*, 3s. 6d.
—— Mrs., *High Alps in Winter*, 14s. See also Main.
BURNLEY, James, *History of Wool and Wool-combing*, 21s.
BURTON, W. K., *Works on Japan*. List on application.
BUTLER, Col. Sir W. F., *Campaign of the Cataracts*, 18s.
—— See also Low's Standard Books.
BUXTON, Ethel M. Wilmot, *Wee Folk*, 5s.
BYNNER. See Low's Standard Novels.
CABLE, G. W., See Low's Standard Novels.

CADOGAN, Lady Adelaide, *Drawing-room Comedies*, illust. 10s. 6d., acting edit. 6d.
—— *Illustrated Games of Patience*, col. diagrams, 12s. 6d.
—— *New Games of Patience*, with coloured diagrams, 12s. 6d.
CAHUN. See Low's Standard Books.
CALDECOTT, Randolph, *Memoir*, by Henry Blackburn, 5s.
—— *Sketches*, pict. bds. 2s. 6d.
CALL, Annie Payson, *Power through Repose*, 3s. 6d.
—— *As a Matter of Course*, 3s. 6d.
CALLAN, H., M.A., *Wanderings on Wheel*, 1s. 6d.
CALVERT, Edward (*artist*), *Memoir*, imp. 4to, 63s. nett.
Cambridge Trifles, 2s. 6d.
Cambridge Staircase, 2s. 6d.
CAMPBELL, Lady Colin, *Book of the Running Brook*, 5s.
CAMPELLO, Count, *Life*, 5s.
CANTERBURY, Archbishop. See Preachers.
Capitals of the World, plates and text, 2 vols., 4to, 63s. nett.
CARBUTT, Mrs., *Five Months Fine Weather ; Canada, &c.*, 5s.
CARLETON, Will, *City Ballads*, illust. 12s. 6d.
—— *City Legends*, ill. 12s. 6d.
—— *Farm Festivals*, ill. 12s. 6d.
——— *City Ballads*, 1s. } 1 vol.,
—— *City Legends*, 1s. } 2s. 6d.
—— *City Festivals*, 1s.
—— *Farm Ballads*, 1s. } 1 vol.
—— *Farm Festivals*, 1s. } 3s. 6d.
—— *Farm Legends*, 1s. }
—— *Poems*, 6 vols. in case, 8s.
—— See also Rose Library.
CARLYLE, T., *Conversations with*, 6s.

CARMICHAEL, H. See Low's Standard Novels.

CARNEGIE, ANDREW, *American Four-in-hand in Britain*, 10s. 6d.; also 1s.

—— *Triumphant Democracy*, 6s.; new edit. 1s. 6d.; paper, 1s.

CAROVÉ, *Story without an End*, illust. by E. V. B., 7s. 6d.

CARPENTER. See Preachers.

CARSON, H. L., *Supreme Court of U.S.* 84s.

CAVE, *Picturesque Ceylon*, 2 vols, 21s. and 28s. nett.

Celebrated Racehorses, fac-sim. portraits, 4 vols., 126s.

CÉLIÈRE. See Low's Standard Books.

Changed Cross, &c., poems, 2s.6d.

Chant-book Companion to the Common Prayer, 2s.; organ ed. 4s.

CHAPIN, *Mountaineering in Colorado*, 10s. 6d.

CHAPLIN, J. G., *Bookkeeping*, 2s. 6d.

CHARLES, J. F. See Playtime Library.

CHARLEY, SIR W., *Crusade against the Constitution*, 7s. 6d.

CHATTOCK, *Notes on Etching*, new edit. 10s. 6d.

CHENEY, A. N., *Fishing with the Fly*, 12s. 6d.

CHERUBINI. See Great Musicians.

Choice Editions of choice books, illustrated by Cope, Creswick, Birket Foster, Horsley, Harrison Weir, &c., 2s. 6d.; re-issue, 1s. each.

Bloomfield's Farmer's Boy.
Campbell's Pleasures of Hope.
Coleridge's Ancient Mariner.
Elizabethan Songs and Sonnets.
Goldsmith's Deserted Village.
Goldsmith's Vicar of Wakefield.
Gray's Elegy in a Churchyard.
Keats' Eve of St. Agnes.

Choice Editions—continued.
Milton's Allegro.
Poetry of Nature, by H. Weir.
Rogers' Pleasures of Memory.
Shakespeare's Songs and Sonnets
Tennyson's May Queen.
Wordsworth's Pastoral Poems.
Chopin, Life of, 10s. 6d.

CHRISTIAN, S., *Lydia*, 2s. 6d.

—— *Sarah*, 2s. 6d.

—— *Two Mistakes*, 3s. 6d.

CHURCH, W. C., *Life of Ericsson*, new ed., 16s.

CHURCHILL, LORD RANDOLPH, *Men, Mines and Animals in South Africa*, 6s.; 2s. 6d.

CLARK, A., *Woe to the Conquered*, 21s.

—— *Dark Place of the Earth*, 6s.

—— Mrs. K. M., *Southern Cross Fairy Tale*, 5s.

—— *Persephone, Poems*, 5s.

CLARKE, PERCY, *Three Diggers*, 6s.

—— *Valley Council;* 6s.

Claude le Lorrain. See Great Artists.

CLIVE BAYLY, *Vignettes from Finland.*

COCHRAN, W., *Pen and Pencil in Asia Minor*, 21s.

COLLINGWOOD, H. See Low's Standard Books.

COLLYER, ROBERT, *Things Old and New*, Sermons, 5s.

CONDER, J., *Flowers of Japan and Decoration*, coloured Plates, 42s. nett.

—— *Landscape Gardening in Japan*, 52s.6d. nett.; supplement. 36s. nett.

CONYBEARE, E., *School Chronology*, 1s.

CORDINGLEY, W. G., *Guide to the Stock Exchange*, 5s.

CORREGGIO. See Great Artists.

COWEN, JOSEPH, M.P., *Life and Speeches*, 14s.

COWPER, F., *Hunting of the Auk*, 5s.

COX, DAVID. See Great Artists.

—— J. CHARLES, *Gardens of Scripture; Meditations*, 5s.

COZZENS, F., *American Yachts*, pfs. 21l.; art. pfs. 31l. 10s.

—— S. W. See Low's Standard Books.

CRADDOCK. See Low's Standard Novels.

CRAIG, W. H., *Dr. Johnson and the Fair Sex.*

CRAIK, D., *Millwright and Miller*, 21s.

CROCKER, *Education of the Horse*, 8s. 6d. nett.

CROKER, MRS. B. M. See Low's Standard Novels.

CROSLAND, MRS. NEWTON, *Landmarks of a Literary Life*, 7s. 6d.

CROUCH, A. P., *Glimpses of Feverland* (West Africa), 6s.

—— *On a Surf-bound Coast*, 7s. 6d.; new edit. 5s.

CRUIKSHANK, G. See Great Artists.

CUDWORTH, W., *Abraham Sharp*, Mathematician, 26s.

CUMBERLAND, STUART. See Low's Standard Novels.

CUNDALL, J., *Shakespeare*, 3s. 6d., and 2s.

—— *History of Wood Engraving*, 2s.

CURTIS, C. B., *Velazquez and Murillo*, with etchings, 31s. 6d.; large paper, 63s.

CUNNINGHAM & ABNEY, *Pioneers of the Alps*, 21s.

—— *Almer's Fuhrerbuch*, 30s.

CUSHING, W., *Anonyms*, 2 vols. 52s. 6d.

CUSHING, W., *Initials and Pseudonyms*, 25s; ser. II., 21s.

CUTCLIFFE, H. C., *Trout Fishing*, new edit. 3s. 6d.

CUTHELL, E. E., *Baireuth Pilgrimage*, 12s.

DALY, MRS. DOMINIC, *Digging, Squatting in N. S. Australia*, 12s.

D'ANVERS, N., *Architecture and Sculpture*, new edit. 5s.

—— *Elementary Art, Architecture, Sculpture, Painting*, new edit. 12s. and 10s. 6d.

—— *Painting*, new ed. by F. Cundall, 6s.

DAUDET, ALPHONSE, *Port Tarascon*, by H. James, 7s. 6d.; also 5s. and 3s. 6d.

DAVIES, C., *Modern Whist*, 4s.

— REV. D., *Talks with Men*, 6s.

DAVIS, C. T., *Manufacture of Leather*, 52s. 6d.

—— *Manufacture of Paper*, 28s.

—— *Manufacture of Bricks* 25s.

—— *Steam Boiler Incrustation*, 8s. 6d.

—— G. B., *International Law*, 10s. 6d.

—— R. H., *Our English Cousins*, 6s.

DAWIDOWSKY, *Glue, Gelatine, Veneers, Cements*, 12s. 6d.

Day of my Life, by an Eton boy, new edit. 2s. 6d.; also 1s.

Days in Clover, by the "Amateur Angler," 1s.; illust., 2s. 6d.

DELLA ROBBIA. See Great Artists.

DEMAGE, G., *Plunge into Sahara*, 5s.

DERRY (B. of). See Preachers.

DE WINT. See Great Artists.

DIGGLE, J. W., *Bishop Fraser's Lancashire Life*, new edit. 12s. 6d.; popular ed. 3s. 6d.

—— *Sermons for Daily Life*, 5s.

8   *A Select List of Books*

DIRUF, O., *Kissingen*, 5s. and 3s. 6d.

DOBSON, AUSTIN, *Hogarth*, illust. 24s.; l. paper 52s. 6d.; new ed. 12s. 6d.

DOD, *Peerage, Baronetage, and Knightage, for 1895*, 10s. 6d.

DODGE, MRS., *Hans Brinker*. See Low's Standard Books.

Doing and Suffering; memorials of E. and F. Bickersteth, 2s. 6d.

DONKIN, J. G., *Trooper and Redskin;* Canada police, 8s. 6d.

DONNELLY, IGNATIUS, *Atlantis, the Antediluvian World*, 12s. 6d.

—— *Cæsar's Column*, authorised edition, 3s. 6d.

—— *Doctor Huguet*, 3s. 6d.

—— *Great Cryptogram*, Bacon's Cipher in the so-called Shakspere Plays, 2 vols., 30s.

—— *Ragnarok: the Age of Fire and Gravel*, 12s. 6d.

DORE, GUSTAVE, *Life and Reminiscences*, by Blanche Roosevelt, fully illust. 24s.

DOUGALL, J. D., *Shooting Appliances, Practice*, n. ed. 7s. 6d.

DOUGLAS, JAMES, *Bombay and Western India*, 2 vols., 42s.

DU CHAILLU, PAUL. See Low's Standard Books.

DUFFY, SIR C. G., *Conversations with Carlyle*, 6s.

DUMAS, A., *Company of Jehu*, 7s.

—— *First Republic*, 7s.

—— *Last Vendée*, 7s.

DUNCKLEY ("Verax.") See Prime Ministers.

DUNDERDALE, GEORGE, *Prairie and Bush*, 6s.

Dürer. See Great Artists.

DYER, T. F., *Strange Pages*, 3s. 6d.

DYKES, J. Osw. See Preachers.

EBERS, G., *Per Aspera*, 2 vols., 21s.; new ed., 2 vols., 4s.

—— *Cleopatra*, 2 vols., 6s.

—— *In the Fire of the Forge*, 2 vols., 6s.

EDMONDS, C., *Poetry of the Anti-Jacobin*, new edit. 7s. 6d.

EDWARDS, *American Steam Engineer*, 12s. 6d.

—— *Modern Locomotive Engines*, 12s. 6d.

—— *Steam Engineer's Guide*, 12s. 6d.

—— M. B., *Dream of Millions, &c.*, 1s.

—— See also Low's Standard Novels.

EDWORDS, *Camp Fires of a Naturalist*, N. Am. Mammals, 6s.

EGGLESTON, G. CARY, *Juggernaut*, 6s.

Egypt. By S. L. POOLE, 3s. 6d.

ELIAS, N., *Tarikh i Rishidi*, 30s. nett.

Elizabethan Songs. See Choice Editions.

ELVEY, SIR GEORGE, *Life*, 8s. 6d.

EMERSON, DR. P. H., *English Idylls*, new ed., 2s.

—— *Pictures of East Anglian Life*, 105s.; large paper, 147s.

—— *Son of the Fens*, 6s.

—— See also Low's 1s. Novels.

—— and GOODALL, *Life on the Norfolk Broads*, plates, 126s.; large paper, 210s.

—— and GOODALL, *Wild Life on a Tidal Water*, copper plates, 25s.; édit. de luxe, 63s.

—— RALPH WALDO, *in Concord*, a memoir by E. W. Emerson, 7s. 6d.

EMERY, G. F., *Guide to Parish Councils Act*, 1d. each.

—— *Parish Councils*, 2s.

EMERY,G. F., *Parish Meetings*, 2s.

English Catalogue, 1872-80, 42s.; 1881-9, 52s. 6d.; 1890-94, 5s. each.

English Catalogue, Index vol. 1856-76, 42s.; 1874-80, 18s.; 1881-89, 31s. 6d.

English Philosophers, edited by E. B. Ivan Müller, 3s. 6d. each. Bacon, by Fowler. Hamilton, by Monck. Hartley and James Mill, by Bower. Shaftesbury & Hutcheson; Fowler. Adam Smith, by J. A. Farrer.

ERCKMANN-CHATRIAN. See Low's Standard Books.

ESLER, E. RENTOUL, *The Way they Loved at Grimpat*, 3s. 6d.

—— *Maid of the Manse*, 3s. 6d.

—— *Mid Green Pastures*, 3s. 6d.

—— *Way of Transgressors.*

ESMARCH, F., *Handbook of Surgery*, with 647 new illust. 24s.

EVANS, G. E., *Repentance of Magdalene Despar, &c.*, poems, 5s.

—— S. & F., *Upper Ten*, a story, 1s.

—— W. E., *Songs of the Birds, Analogies of Spiritual Life*, 6s.

EVELYN. See Low's Stand. Books.

—— JOHN, *Life of Mrs. Godolphin*, 7s. 6d.

EVES, C. W., *West Indies*, n. ed. 7s. 6d.

Explorers of Africa, 2 vols., 25s.

EYRE-TODD, *Anne of Argyle*, 6s.

FAGAN, L., *History of Engraving in England*, illust. from rare prints, £25 nett.

FAIRBAIRN. See Preachers.

Faith and Criticism; Essays by Congregationalists, 6s.

Familiar Words. See Gentle Life Series.

FARINI, G. A., *Through the Kalahari Desert*, 21s.

Farragut, Admiral, by Capt. Mahan, 6s.

FAWCETT, *Heir to Millions*, 6s.

—— *American Push*, 6s.

—— See also Rose Library.

FAY, T., *Three Germanys*, 2 vols. 35s.

FEILDEN, H. ST. J., *Some Public Schools*, 2s. 6d.

—— Mrs., *My African Home*, 7s. 6d.

FENN, G. MANVILLE. *Black Bar*, illust. 5s., 3s. 6d. and 2s. 6d.

—— *Fire Island*, 6s.

—— See also Low's Stand. Bks

FFORDE, B., *Subaltern, Policeman, and the Little Girl*, 1s.

— *Trotter, a Poona Mystery*, 1s.

FIELDS, JAMES T., *Memoirs*, 12s. 6d.

—— *Yesterdays with Authors*, 10s. 6d.

FINCK, HENRY T., *Pacific Coast Scenic Tour*, fine pl. 10s. 6d.

FISHER, G. P., *Colonial Era in America*, 7s. 6d.

FITZGERALD, PERCY, *Book Fancier,* 5.; large paper, 12s. 6d.

FITZPATRICK, T., *Autumn Cruise in the Ægean*, 10s. 6d.

—— *Transatlantic Holiday*, 10s. 6d.

FLEMING, S., *England and Canada*, 6s.

FLETCHER, *Public Libaries in America*, 3s. 6d.

Fly Fisher's Register of Date, Place, Time Occupied, &c., 4s.

FOLKARD, R., *Plant Lore, Legends and Lyrics*, n. ed., 10s. 6d.

FOREMAN, J., *Philippine Islands*, 21s.

FOSTER, B., *Some Places of Note*, 63s.

—— F. P., *Medical Dictionary*, 180s. nett.

FRANC, MAUD JEANNE, *Beatrice Melton*, 4s.

—— *Emily's Choice*, n. ed. 5s.

—— *Golden Gifts*, 4s.

—— *Hall's Vineyard*, 4s.

—— *Into the Light*, 4s.

—— *John's Wife*, 4s.

—— *Little Mercy;* 4s.

—— *Marian, a Tale*, n. ed. 5s.

—— *Master of Ralston*, 4s.

—— *Minnie's Mission*, 4s.

—— *No longer a Child*, 4s.

—— *Silken Cords*, a Tale, 4s.

—— *Two Sides to Every Question*, 4s.

—— *Vermont Vale*, 5s.
A plainer edition is issued at 2s. 6d.

Frank's Ranche; or, My Holiday in the Rockies, n. ed. 5s.

FRASER, Sir W. A., *Hic et ubique*, 3s. 6d.; large paper, 21s.

FREEMAN, J., *Melbourne Life*, lights and shadows, 6s.

French and English Birthday Book, by Kate D. Clark, 7s. 6d.

French Readers. See Low.

Fresh Woods and Pastures New, by the Amateur Angler, 1s. 6d.

FRIEZE, *Dupré, Florentine Sculptor*, 7s. 6d.

FRISWELL. See Gentle Life.

Froissart for Boys. See Lanier.

FROUDE, J. A. See Prime Ministers.

FRY, H., *History of North Atlantic Navigation*, 7s. 6d.

Gainsborough and Constable. See Great Artists.

GARLAND, HAMLIN, *Prairie Folks*, 6s.

GASPARIN, *Sunny Fields and Shady Woods*, 6s.

GEFFCKEN, *British Empire*, translated, 7s. 6d.

Gentle Life Series, edited by J. Hain Friswell, 16mo, 2s. 6d. each.

Gentle Life.
About in the World.
Like unto Christ.
Familiar Words, 6s.; also 3s. 6d.
Montaigne's Essays.
Gentle Life, second series.
Silent hour; essays.
Half-length Portraits.
Essays on English Writers.
Other People's Windows, 6s. & 2s. 6d.
A Man's Thoughts.

GESSI, ROMOLO PASHA, *Seven Years in the Soudan*, 18s.

GHIBERTI & DONATELLO
See Great Artists.

GIBBS, W. A., *Idylls of the Queen*, 1s., 5s., & 3s.; Prelude, 1s.

GIBSON, W. H., *Happy Hunting Grounds*, 31s. 6d.

GILES, E., *Australia Twice Traversed*, 1872-76, 2 vols. 30s.

GILL, J. See Low's Readers.

GILLIAT. See Low's Stand. Novels.

Giotto, by Harry Quilter, illust. 15s. See also Great Artists.

GLADSTONE, W. E. See Prime Ministers.

GLAVE, E. J., *Congoland, Six Years' Adventure*, 7s. 6d.

Goethe's Faustus, in the original rhyme, by Alfred H. Huth, 5s.

—— *Prosa*, by C. A. Buchheim (Low's German Series), 3s. 6d.

GOLDSMITH, O., *She Stoops to Conquer*, by Austin Dobson, illust. by E. A. Abbey, 8s.

—— See also Choice Editions.

GOOCH, FANNY C., *Face to Face with the Mexicans*, 16s.

GOODMAN, E. J., *The Best Tour in Norway*, new edit., 7s. 6d.

GOODYEAR, W. H., *Grammar of the Lotus, Ornament and Sun Worship*, 63s. nett.

GORDON, E. A., *Clear Round, Story from other Countries*, 7s. 6d.

—— J. E. H., *Physical Treatise on Electricity and Magnetism*, 3rd ed. 2 vols. 42s.

—— *School Electricity*, 5s.

—— Mrs. J. E. H., *Decorative Electricity*, illust. 12s.; n. ed. 6s.

—— *Eunice Anscombe*, 7s. 6d.

GOUFFÉ, *Cookery Book*, 10s. 6d.

GOUGH, E. J. See Preachers.

Gounod. Life and Works, 10s. 6d.

GOWER, LORD RONALD. See Great Artists.

GRAESSI, *Italian Dictionary*, 3s. 6d.; roan, 5s.

Grant, General, Memoirs, 6s.

Great Artists, Illustrated Biographies, 2s. 6d. per vol. except where the price is given.

Barbizon School, 2 vols.
Claude le Lorrain.
Correggio, 2s.
Cox and De Wint.
George Cruikshank.
Della Robbia and Cellini, 2s.
Albrecht Dürer.
Figure Painters of Holland. By Lord Ronald Gower.
Fra Angelico, Masaccio, &c.
Fra Bartolommeo; Leader Scott.
Gainsborough and Constable.
Ghiberti and Donatello, by Leader Scott, 2s. 6d.
Giotto, by H. Quilter; 4to, 15s.
Hogarth, by Austin Dobson.
Hans Holbein.
Landscape Painters of Holland.
Landseer, by F. G. Stephens.
Leonardo da Vinci, by J P. Richter.

Great Artists—continued.

Little Masters of Germany, by W. B. Scott; éd. de luxe, 10s. 6d.
Mantegna and Francia.
Meissonier, 2s.
Michelangelo.
Mulready.
Murillo, by Ellen E. Minor, 2s.
Overbeck, by J. B. Atkinson.
Raphael, by N. D'Anvers.
Rembrandt, by J. W. Mollett.
Reynolds, by F. S. Pulling.
Romney and Lawrence, 2s.
Rubens, by Kett.
Tintoretto, by Osler.
Titian, by Heath.
Turner, by Monkhouse.
Vandyck and Hals, by P. R. Head.
Velasquez, by Edwin Stowe.
Vernet & Delaroche.
Watteau, by Mollett, 2s.
Wilkie, by Mollett.

Great Musicians, biographies, edited by F. Hueffer, 3s. each:—
Bach.   Mozart.
Beethoven.   Purcell.
Cherubini.   Rossini.
English Church   Schubert.
 Composers.   Schumann.
Handel.   Richard Wagner.
Haydn.   Weber.
Mendelssohn.

GRIEB, *German Dictionary*, n. ed. 2 vols., fine paper, cloth, 21s.

"GRINGO," *Land of the Aztecs*, 6s.

GROHMANN, *Camps in the Rockies*, 12s. 6d.

GROVES. See Low's Std. Bks.

GUILLÉ. *Instruction and Amusements of the Blind*, ill., 5s.

GUIZOT, *History of England*, illust. 3 vols. re-issue, 10s. 6d. ea.

—— *History of France*, illust. re-issue, 8 vols. 10s. 6d. each.

—— Abridged by G. Masson, 5s.

GUNN, E. S., *Romance of Paradise*, 3s. 6d.

GUYON, Madame, *Life*, 6s.

HADLEY, J., *Roman Law*, 7s. 6d.

HALE, *How to Tie Salmon-Flies*, 12s. 6d.

HALFORD, F. M., *Dry Fly-fishing*, n. ed. 25s. nett.

—— *Floating Flies*, 15s.

HALL, *How to Live Long*, 2s.

HALSEY, F. A., *Slide Valve Gears*, 8s. 6d.

HAMILTON. See English Philosophers.

—— E. *Fly-fishing for Salmon*, 6s. ; large paper, 10s. 6d.

—— *Riverside Naturalist*, 14s.

—— J. A., *Mountain Path*, 3s. 6d.

HANCOCK, H., *Mechanics*, 5s.

HANDEL. See G. Musicians.

HANDS, T., *Numerical Exercises in Chemistry*, 2s. 6d.

Handy Guide to Dry-fly Fishing, by Cotswold Isys, new ed., 1s.

Handy Guide Book to Japanese Islands, 6s. 6d.

HARKUT. See Low's Stand. Novels.

HARRIS, J., *Evening Tales*, 6s.

—— W. B., *Land of an African Sultan*, 10s. 6d., 5s., and 2s. 6d.

HARRISON, Mary, *Modern Cookery*, 6s. and 3s. 6d.

—— *Skilful Cook*, n. ed. 3s. 6d.

—— W., *London Houses*, Illust. n. edit., 2s. 6d.

—— *Memor. Paris Houses*, 6s.

HATTON. See Low's Standard Novels.

HAWEIS, H.R., *Broad Church*, 6s.

—— *Poets in the Pulpit*, new edit. 6s. ; also 3s. 6d.

—— Mrs., *Housekeeping*, 2s. 6d.

—— *Beautiful Houses*, n. ed. 1s.

HAYDN. See Great Musicians.

HAZLITT. See Bayard Ser.

HEAD, Percy R. See Illus. Text Books and Great Artists.

HEARN, L., *Youma*, 5s.

HEATH, Gertrude, *Tell us Why*, 2s. 6d.

HEGINBOTHAM, *Stockport*, I., II., III., IV., V., 10s. 6d. each.

HELDMANN, B. See Low's Standard Books for Boys.

HENTY, G. A. See Low's Standard Books for Boys.

—— Richmond, *Australiana*, 5s.

HERNDON, W. H., *Life of A. Lincoln*, 2 vols. 12s.

HERRICK, R., *Poetry Edited by Austin Dobson*, illust. by E. A. Abbey, 42s.

HERVEY, Gen., *Records of Crime, Thuggee, &c.*, 2 vols., 30s.

HICKS, C. S., *Our Boys, and what to do with Them; Merchant Service*, 5s.

—— *Yachts, Boats, and Canoes, Design and Construction*, 10s. 6d.

HILL, G. B., *Footsteps of Johnson*, 63s. ; édition de luxe, 147s.

—— Katharine St., *Grammar of Palmistry*, new ed., 1s.

HINMAN, R., *Eclectic Physical Geography*, 5s.

Hints on proving Wills without Professional Assistance, n. ed. 1s.

Historic Bindings in the Bodleian Library, many plates, 94s. 6d., 84s., 52s. 6d. and 42s.

HODDER, E., *History of South Australia*, 2 vols., 24s.

HOEY, Mrs. Cashel. See Low's Standard Novels.

HOFFER, *Caoutchouc & Gutta Percha*, by W. T. Brannt, 12s. 6d.

HOFFMAN, C., *Paper Making*, 100s.

HOGARTH. See Gr. Artists, and Dobson, Austin.

HOLBEIN. See Great Artists.

HOLDER, CHARLES F., *Ivory King*, 8s. 6d.; now ed. 3s. 6d.

—— *Living Lights*, n. ed. 3s. 6d.

HOLLINGSHEAD, J., *My Life Time*. 2 vols., 21s.

HOLMAN, T., *Life in the Royal Navy*, 1s.

—— *Salt Yarns*, new ed., 1s.

HOLMES, O. WENDELL, *Before the Curfew*, 5s.

—— *Guardian Angel*, 2s. and 2s. 6d.

—— *Over the Tea Cups*, 6s.

—— *Iron Gate*, &c., *Poems*, 6s.

—— *Last Leaf*, holiday vol., 42s.

—— *Mechanism in Thought and Morals*, 1s. 6d.

—— *Mortal Antipathy*, 8s. 6d., 2s. and 1s.

—— *Our Hundred Days in Europe*, new edit. 6s., 3s. 6d., and 2s. 6d., large paper, 15s.

—— *Poetical Works*, new edit., 2 vols. 10s. 6d.

—— *Works*, prose, 10 vols. ; poetry, 3 vols.; 13 vols. 84s.

—— See also Low's Standard Novels and Rose Library.

Homer, Iliad, translated by A. Way, vol. I., 9s.; II., 9s.; Odyssey, in English verse, 7s. 6d.

Horace in Latin, with Smart's literal translation , 2s. 6d. ; translation only, 1s. 6d.

HOSMER, J., *German Literature*, a short history, 7s. 6d.

How and where to Fish in Ireland, by Hi-Regan, 3s. 6d.

HOWARD, BLANCHE W., *Tony the Maid*, 3s. 6d.

—— See also Low's Standard Novels.

HOWELLS, W.D. *Undiscovered Country*, 3s. 6d. and 1s.

HOWORTH, SIR H. H., *Glacial Nightmare & the Flood*, 2 vols., 30s.

—— *Mammoth and the Flood*, 18s.

HUEFFER. F. See Great Musicians.

HUGHES, HUGH PRICE. See Preachers.

—— W., *Dark Africa*, 2s.

HUGO'S *Notre Dame*, 10s. 6d.

HUME, FERGUS, *Creature of the Night*, 1s. See also Low's Standard Novels and 1s. Novels.

HUMFREY, MARIAN, *Obstetric Nursing*, 2 vols., 3s. 6d. each.

Humorous Art at the Naval Exhibition, 1s.

HUMPHREYS, JENNET, *Some Little Britons in Brittany*, 2s. 6d.

HUNTINGDON, *The Squire's Nieces*, 2s. 6d. (Playtime Library.)

HYDE, *A Hundred Years by Post*, Jubilee Retrospect, 1s.

HYNE, G. J., *Sandy Carmichael*, 5s., 3s. 6d., and 2s. 6d.

Hymnal Companion to the Book of Common Prayer, separate lists gratis.

Illustrated Text-Books of Art-Education, edit. by E. J. Poynter, R.A., 5s. each.

Architecture, Classic and Early Christian, by Smith and Slater.

Architecture, Gothic and Renaissance, by T. Roger Smith.

German, Flemish, and Dutch Painting.

Painting, Classic and Italian, by Head, &c.

Painting, English and American.

Sculpture, modern ; Leader Scott.

Sculpture, by G. Redford.

Spanish and French artists ; Smith.

Water Colour Painting, by Redgrave.

INDERWICK, F. A., *Inter-regnum*, 10s. 6d.

—— *Prisoner of War*, 5s.

—— *King Edward and New Winchelsea*, 10s. 6d.

—— *Sidelights on the Stuarts*, new edit. 7s. 6d.

INGELOW, JEAN. See Low's Standard Novels.

INGLIS, HON. JAMES, *Our New Zealand Cousins*, 6s.

—— *Sport and Work on the Nepaul Frontier*, 21s.

—— *Tent Life in Tiger Land*, with coloured plates, 18s.

IRVING, W., *Little Britain*, 10s. 6d. and 6s.

JACKSON, John, *Compendium*, 1s.

—— *New Style Vertical Writing Copy-Books*, 1—15, 2d. each.

—— *New Code Copy-Books*, 25 Nos. 2d. each.

—— *Shorthand of Arithmetic*, Companion to Arithmetics, 1s. 6d.

—— *Theory and Practice of Handwriting*, with diagrams, 5s.

JALKSON, LOWIS, *Ten Centuries of European Progress*, 3s. 6d.

JAMES, CROAKE, *Law and Lawyers*, new edit. 7s. 6d.

JAMES and MOLÉ'S *French Dictionary*, 3s. 6d. cloth; roan, 5s.

JAMES, *German Dictionary*, 3s. 6d. cloth; roan, 5s.

JANVIER, *Aztec Treasure House*. See also Low's Standard Books.

Japanese Books, untearable.
1. Rat's Plaint, by Little, 5s.
2. Smith, Children's Japan, 3s. 6d.
3. Bramhall, Niponese Rhymes, 5s.
4. Princess Splendor, fairy tale. 2s.

JEFFERIES, RICHARD, *Amaryllis at the Fair*, 7s. 6d.

—— See also Low's Stan. Books.

JEFFERSON, R. L., *A Wheel to Moscow*, 2s. 6d.

JEPHSON, A. J. M., *Emin Pasha* relief expedition, 21s.

—— *Stories told in an African Forest*, 8s. 6d.

JOHNSTON, H. H., *The Congo, from its Mouth to Bólóbó*, 21s. and 2s. 6d.

JOHNSTON-LAVIS, H. J., *South Italian Volcanoes*, 15s.

JOHNSTONE, D. L., *Land of the Mountain Kingdom*, 2s. 6d.

JOINVILLE. See Bayard Ser.

JONES, REV. J. M. See Preachers.

JULIEN, F., *Conversational French Reader*, 2s. 6d.

—— *English Student's French Examiner*, 2s.

—— *First Lessons in Conversational French Grammar*, n. ed. 1s.

—— *French at Home and at School*, Book I. accidence, 2s.; key, 3s.

—— *Petites Leçons de Conversation et de Grammaire*, n. ed. 3s.

—— *Petites Leçons*, with phrases, 3s. 6d.

—— *Phrases of Daily Use*, separately, 6d.

KARR, H. W. SETON, *Shores and Alps of Alaska*, 16s.

Keene (C.), Life, by Layard, 24s.; l.p., 63s. nett; n. ed., 12s. 6d.

KENNEDY, E. B., *Blacks and Bushrangers*, 5s., 3s. 6d., and 2s. 6d.

—— *Out of the Groove*, 6s.

KERSHAW, S. W., *Protestants from France in their English Home*, 6s.

KILNER, E. A., *Four Welsh Counties*, 5s.

KINGSLEY, R. G., *Children of Westminster Abbey*, 5s.

KINGSTON, W. H. G. See Low's Standard Books.

KIRKALDY, W. G., *David Kirkaldy's Mechanical Testing*, 84s.

KNIGHT, E. F., *Cruise of the Falcon*, 7s. 6d.; new edit. 2s. 6d.

KNOX, T. W., *Boy Travellers with H. M. Stanley*, new edit. 5s.

——*John Boyd's Adventures*, 6s.

KRUMMACHER, *Dictionary Everyday German*, 5s.

KUNHARDT, C. P., *Small Yachts*, new edit. 50s.

—— *Steam Yachts*, 16s.

KWONG, *English Phrases*, 21s.

LABILLIERE, *Federal Britain*, 6s.

Lafayette, General, Life, 12s.

LALANNE, *Etching*, 12s. 6d.

LAMB, CHAS., *Essays of Elia*, with designs by C. O. Murray, 6s.

Landscape Painters of Holland. See Great Artists.

LANDSEER. See Great Artists.

LANGE, P., *Pictures of Norway*, 52s. 6d.

LANIER, S., *Boy's Froissart*, 7s. 6d.; *King Arthur*, 7s. 6d.; *Percy*, 7s. 6d.

LANSDELL, HENRY, *Through Siberia*, 2 vols., 30s.

—— *Russian Central Asia*, 2 vols. 42s.

—— *Through Central Asia*, 12s.

—— *Chinese Central Asia*, 2 vols., fully illustrated, 36s.

LARDEN, W., *School Course on Heat*, 5th ed., entirely revised, 5s.

LARNED, W. C., *Churches and Castles*, 10s. 6d.

LAURENCE, SERGEANT, *Autobiography*, 6s.

LAURIE, A. See Low's Stand. Books.

LAWRENCE. See Romney in Great Artists.

LAYARD, MRS., *West Indies*, 2s. 6d.

——G.S., *His Golf Madness*, 1s.

—— See also Keene.

LEA, H. C., *Inquisition in the Middle Ages*, 3 vols., 42s.

LEANING, J., *Specifications*, 4s.

LEARED, A., *Morocco*, n. ed. 16s.

LEECH, H. J., *John Bright's Letters*, 5s.

LEFFINGWELL, W. B., *Shooting*, 18s.

—— *Wild Fowl Shooting*, 10s. 6d.

LEFROY, W., DEAN OF NORWICH. See Preachers of the Age.

LEIBBRAND, DR., *This Age Ours*, 6s.

Leo XIII. Life, 18s.

Leonardo da Vinci. See Great Artists.

—— *Literary Works*, by J. P. Richter, 2 vols. 252s.

LEVETT YEATS, S. See Low's Standard Novels.

LIEBER, *Telegraphic Cipher*, 42s. nett.

Like unto Christ. See Gentle Life Series.

Lincoln, Abraham, true story of a great life, 2 vols., 12s.

LITTLE, ARCH. J., *Yang-tse Gorges*, n. ed., 10s. 6d.

—— See also Japanese Books.

LITTLE, W. J. KNOX-. See Preachers of the Age.

Little Masters of Germany. See Great Artists.

LODGE, *Life of George Washington*, 12s.

LOFTIE, W. J., *Orient Line Guide*, 3s. 6d.

LONG, JAMES, *Farmer's Handbook*, 4s. 6d.

LONGFELLOW, *Maidenhood*, with coloured plates, 2s. 6d.
—— *Nuremberg*, photogravure illustrations, 31s. 6d.
—— *Song of Hiawatha*, 21s.
LOOMIS, E., *Astronomy*, 8s. 6d.
LORD, Mrs. FREWEN, *Tales from Westminster Abbey*, 2s. 6d.; new edition, 1s.
—— *Tales from St. Paul's*, 1s.
LORNE, MARQUIS OF, *Canada and Scotland*, 7s. 6d.
—— See also Prime Ministers.
Louis, St. See Bayard Series.
Low's Chemical Lecture Charts, 31s. 6d.
—— *French Readers*, ed. by C. F. Clifton, I. 3d., II. 3d., III. 6d.
—— *German Series.* See Goethe, Meissner, Sandars, and Schiller.
—— *London Charities*, annually, 1s. 6d.; sewed, 1s.
——*Illustrated Germ. Primer*, 1s.
—— *Infant Primers*, I. illus. 3d.; II. illus. 6d.
—— *Pocket Encyclopædia*, with plates, 3s. 6d.; roan, 4s. 6d.
—— *Readers*, Edited by John Gill, I., 9d.; II., 10d.; III., 1s.; IV., 1s. 3d.; V., 1s. 4d.; VI., 1s. 6d.
Low's Stand. Library of Travel and Adventure. 2s. 6d. per vol.
Ashe (R. P.), Two Kings of Uganda; also 3s. 6d.
Butler (Sir W. F.) The Great Lone Land: A Record of Travel and Adventure in North and West America.
Churchill (Lord R.), Men, Mines, and Animals in South Africa.
Harris (W. B.), The Land of an African Sultan: Travels in Morocco.
Holmes (Dr. O. W.), Our Hundred Days in Europe.

Low's Stand. Library of Travel—continued.
Johnston (H. H.), The River Congo, from its Mouth to Bólóbó.
Knight (E. F.), Cruise of the *Falcon*: A Voyage to South America in a Thirty-Ton Yacht; also 3s. 6d.
Spry (W. J. J.), The Cruise of the *Challenger*; also 7s. 6d.
Stanley (H. M.) How I Found Livingstone; also 3s. 6d.
Wingate (Major F. R.), Ten Years' Captivity in the Mahdi's Camp, 1882-1892; also 6s.
Other Volumes in preparation.

Low's Standard Novels, Library Edition (except where price is stated), cr. 8vo., 6s.; also popular edition (marked with *), small post 8vo, 2s. 6d.
Baker, John Westacott, 3s. 6d.
—— Mark Tillotson.
*Black (William) Adventures in Thule.
*—— The Beautiful Wretch.
*—— Daughter of Heth.
*—— Donald Ross of Heimra.
*—— Green Pastures & Piccadilly.
—— The Handsome Humes.
—— Highland Cousins.
*—— In Far Lochaber.
*—— In Silk Attire.
*—— Judith Shakespeare.
*—— Kilmeny.
*——Lady Silverdale's Sweetheart
*—— Macleod of Dare.
*—— Madcap Violet.
—— The Magic Ink.
*—— Maid of Killeena.
*—— New Prince Fortunatus.
*—— The Penance of John Logan.
*—— Princess of Thule.
*—— Sabina Zembra.
*—— Shandon Bells.
*—— Stand Fast, Craig Royston!
*—— Strange Adventures of a House Boat.
*—— Strange Adventures of a Phaeton.
*—— Sunrise.
*—— Three Feathers.

Low's Stand. Novels—continued.

Stoker (Bram) Snake's Pass.
Stowe (Mrs.) Poganuc People.
Thanet (O.), Stories of a Western
　Town.
Thomas, House on the Scar.
Thomson (Joseph) Ulu.
Tourgee, Murvale Eastman.
Tytler (S.) Duchess Frances.
*Vane, From the Dead.
—— Polish Conspiracy.
*Walford (Mrs.), Her Great Idea.
Warner, Little Journey in the World.
Wilcox, Senora Villena.
Woolson (Constance F.) Anne.
—— East Angels.
—— For the Major, 5s
—— Jupiter Lights.
Yeats (S. L.), Honour of Savelli.

Low's Shilling Novels.

Edwards, Dream of Millions.
Emerson, East Coast Yarns.
—— Signor Lippo.
Evans, Upper Ten.
Forde, Subaltern, &c.
—— Trotter : a Poona Mystery.
Hewitt, Oriel Penhaligon.
Holman, Life in the Royal Navy.
—— Salt Yarns.
Hume (F.), Creature of the Night.
—— Chinese Jar.
Ignotus; Visitors' Book.
Layard, His Golf Madness.
Married by Proxy.
Rux, Roughing it after Gold.
—— Through the Mill.
Vane, Lynn's Court Mystery.
Vesper, Bobby, a Story.

Low's Standard Books for Boys,
　with   numerous   illustrations,
　2s. 6d. each ; gilt edges, 3s. 6d.

Ainslie, Priceless Orchid.
Biart (Lucien) Young Naturalist.
—— My Rambles in the New World.
Boussenard, Crusoes of Guiana.
—— Gold Seekers, a sequel.
Butler (Col. Sir Wm.) Red Cloud.
Cahun (Leon) Captain Mago.
—— Blue Banner.
Célière, Exploits of the Doctor.

Low's Stand. Books for Boys—continued.

Collingwood, Under the Meteor Flag
—— Voyage of the *Aurora*.
Cozzens (S. W.) Marvellous Country.
Dodge (Mrs.) Hans Brinker.
Du Chaillu (Paul) Gorilla Country.
—— Wild Life on the Equator.
Erckmann-Chatrian, Bros. Rantzau.
Evelyn, Inca Queen.
Fenn (G. Manville) Off to the Wilds.
—— Silver Cañon.
—— The Black Bar.
Groves (Percy) Charmouth Grange.
Heldmann (B.) *Leander* Mutiny.
Henty (G. A.) Cornet of Horse.
—— Jack Archer.
—— Winning his Spurs.
Hyne, Sandy Carmichael.
Janvier, Aztec Treasure House.
Jefferies (Richard) Bevis, Story of
　a Boy.
Johnstone, Mountain Kingdom.
Kennedy, Blacks and Bushrangers.
Kingston (W. H. G.) Ben Burton.
—— Captain Mugford.
—— Dick Cheveley.
—— Heir of Kilfinnan.
—— Snowshoes and Canoes.
—— Two Supercargoes.
—— With Axe and Rifle.
Laurie (A.) Axel Ebersen.
—— Conquest of the Moon.
—— New York to Brest.
—— Secret of the Magian.
MacGregor (John) *Rob Roy* Canoe.
—— *Rob Roy* in the Baltic.
—— Yawl *Rob Roy*.
Maelean, Maid of the *Golden Age*.
Mael, P., Under the Sea to the
　Pole.
Malan (A. N.) Cobbler of Corni-
　keranium.
Mennier, Great Hunting Grounds.
Muller, Noble Words and Deeds.
Norway (G.) How Martin Drake
　found his Father.
Perelaer, The Three Deserters.
Reed (Talbot Baines) Roger Ingle-
　ton, Minor.
—— Sir Ludar.
Reid (Mayne) Strange Adventures.

Low's Stand. Books for Boys—continued.
Rousselet (Louis) Drummer-boy.
—— King of the Tigers.
—— Serpent Charmer.
—— Son of the Constable.
Russell (W. Clark) Frozen Pirate.
Stanley, My Kalulu.
Tregance, Louis, in New Guinea.
Van Hare, Life of a Showman.
Verne, Adrift in the Pacific.
—— Cæsar Cascabel.
—— Family without a Name.
—— Purchase of the North Pole.
Winder (F. H.) Lost in Africa.

Low's Standard Series of Girls' Books by popular writers, cloth gilt, 2s.; gilt edges, 2s. 6d. each.
Alcott (L. M.) A Rose in Bloom.
—— An Old-Fashioned Girl.
—— Aunt Jo's Scrap Bag.
—— Eight Cousins, illust.
—— Jack and Jill.
—— Jimmy's Cruise.
—— Little Men.
—— Little Women & L.Wo.Wedded
—— Lulu's Library, illust.
—— Recollections of Childhood.
—— Shawl Straps.
—— Silver Pitchers.
—— Spinning-Wheel Stories.
—— Under the Lilacs, illust.
—— Work and Beginning Again, ill.
Alden (W. L.) Jimmy Brown, illust.
—— Trying to Find Europe.
Bunyan, Pilgrim's Progress, 2s.
De Witt (Madame) An Only Sister.
Franc (Maud J.), Stories, 2s. 6d. edition, see page 9.
Holm (Saxe) Draxy Miller's Dowry.
Robinson (Phil) Indian Garden.
—— Under the Punkah.
Roe (E. P.) Nature's Serial Story.
Saintine, Picciola.
Samuels, Forecastle to Cabin, illust.
Sandeau (Jules) Seagull Rock.
Stowe (Mrs.) Dred.
—— Ghost in the Mill, &c.
—— Minister's Wooing.
—— My Wife and I.
—— We and our Neighbours.

Low's Standard Series of Books for Girls—continued.
Tooley (Mrs.) Harriet B. Stowe.
Warner, In the Wilderness.
—— My Summer in a Garden.
Whitney (Mrs.) Leslie Goldthwaite.
—— Faith-Gartney's Girlhood.
—— The Gayworthys.
—— Hitherto.
—— Real Folks.
—— We Girls.
—— The Other Girls: a Sequel.
*** *A new illustrated list of books for boys and girls, with portraits, sent post free on application.*

LOWELL, J. R., *Among my Books*, I. and II., 7s. 6d. each.
—— *Vision of Sir Launfal*, illus. 63s.
LUMMIS, C. F., *Tramp, Ohio to California*, 6s.
—— *Land of Poco Tiempo* (New Mexico), 10s. 6d., illust.
MACDONALD, D., *Oceania*, 6s.
—— *Sweet Scented Flowers*, 5s.
—— GEORGE. See Low's Stand. Novels.
—— SIR JOHN A., *Life*, 16s.
MACGOUN, *Commercial Correspondence*, 5s.
MACGREGOR, J., *Rob Roy in the Baltic*, n. ed. 3s. 6d. and 2s. 6d.
—— *Rob Roy Canoe*, new edit., 3s. 6d. and 2s. 6d.
—— *Yawl Rob Roy*, new edit., 3s. 6d. and 2s. 6d.
MACKENNA, *Brave Men in Action*, 10s. 6d.
MACKENZIE, SIR MORELL, *Fatal Illness of Frederick the Noble*, 2s. 6d.
—— *Essays*, 7s. 6d.
MACKINNON and SHADBOLT, S. *African Campaign*, 50s.
MACLAREN, A. See Preachers.
MACLEAN, H. E. See Low's Standard Books.

MACMASTER. See Low's Standard Novels.

MACMULLEN, J. M., *History of Canada*, 3rd ed., 2 vols., 25s.

MACMURDO, E., *History of Portugal*, 3 vols., 21s. each.

MAEL, PIERRE, *Under the Sea to the North Pole*, 5s. and 2s. 6d.

MAHAN, CAPT. A. T., *Admiral Farragut*, 6s.

—— *Influence of Sea Power on the French Revolution*, 2 vols. (British naval history), 30s.

—— *Sea Power in History*, 18s.

MAIN, MRS., *My Home in the Alps*, 3s. 6d.

—— *Hints on Snow Photography*, 1s. 6d.

—— See also Burnaby, Mrs.

MALAN. See Low's Stand. Books

—— C. F. DE M., *Eric and Connie's Cruise*, 5s.

Manchester Library, Reprints of Classics, per vol., 6d.; sewed, 3d. List on application.

MANLEY, *Notes on Fish and Fishing*, 6s.

MANTEGNA and FRANCIA. See Great Artists.

MARBURY, *Favourite Flies*, with coloured plates, &c., 24s. nett.

MARCH, F. A., *Comparative Anglo-Saxon Grammar*, 12s.

—— *Anglo-Saxon Reader*, 7s. 6d.

MARKHAM, ADM., *Naval Career during the old war*, 14s.

—— CLEMENTS R., *War Between Peru and Chili*, 10s. 6d.

MARSH, A. E. W., *Holiday in Madeira*, 5s.

—— G. P., *Lectures on the English Language*, 18s.

—— *Origin and History of the English Language*, 18s.

MARSHALL, W. G., *Through America*, new edit. 7s. 6d.

MARSTON, E., *How Stanley wrote "In Darkest Africa,"* 1s.

—— See also Amateur Angler, Frank's Ranche, and Fresh Woods.

—— R. B., *Walton and Some Earlier Angling Writers*, 4s. 6d.

—— See also Walton's "Compleat Angler."

—— WESTLAND, *Eminent Recent Actors*, n. ed., 6s.

MARTIN, J. W., *Float Fishing and Spinning*, new edit. 2s.

MATHESON, ANNIE, *Love's Music, and other lyrics*, 3s. 6d.

MATTHEWS, J. W., *Incwadi Yami, 20 Years in S. Africa*, 14s.

MAUCHLINE, ROBERT, *Mine Foreman's Handbook*, 21s.

MAURY, M. F., *Life*, 12s. 6d.

MAURY, M. F., *Physical Geography and Meteorology of the Sea*, new ed. 6s.

MAURY, GENL. H., *Recollections*, 7s. 6d.

MEISSNER, A. L., *Children's Own German Book* (Low's Series), 1s. 6d.

—— *First German Reader* (Low's Series), 1s. 6d.

—— *Second German Reader* (Low's Series), 1s. 6d.

MEISSONIER. See Great Artists.

MELBOURNE, LORD. See Prime Ministers.

MELIO, G. L., *Swedish Drill*, entirely new edition, 2s. 6d.

Member for Wrottenborough, by ARTHUR A'BECKETT, 3s. 6d.

Men of Achievement, 8s. 6d. each.
Noah Brooks, *Statesmen*.
Gen. A. W. Greeley, *Explorers*.
Philip G. Hubert, *Inventors*.
W. O. Stoddard, *Men of Business*.

MENDELSSOHN. *Family,* 1729-1847, Letters and Journals, new edit., 2 vols., 30*s*.

——— See also Great Musicians.

MERIWETHER, LEE, *Mediterranean*, new ed., 6*s*.

MERRYLEES, J., *Carlsbad,* new edition, 3*s*. 6*d*.

MERRIFIELD, J., *Nautical Astronomy*, 7*s*. 6*d*.

MESNEY,W., *Tungking*,3*s*. 6*d*.

Metal Workers' Recipes and Processes, by W. T. Brannt, 12*s*.6*d*.

MEUNIER, V. See Low's Standard Books.

Michelangelo. See Great Artists.

MIJATOVICH, C., *Constantine*, 7*s*. 6*d*.

MILL, JAMES. See English Philosophers.

MILLS, J., *Alternative Chemistry*, answers to the ordinary course, 1*s*.

——— *Alternative Elementary Chemistry*, 1*s*. 6*d*. ; answers, 1*s*.

——— J., *Chemistry for students*, 3*s*. 6*d*.

MILNE, J., AND BURTON, *Volcanoes of Japan*, collotypes by Ogawa, part i., 21*s*. nett.

MITCHELL, D.G.(Ik. Marvel) *English Lands, Letters and Kings,* 2 vols. 6*s*. each.

——— *Writings*, new edit. per vol. 5*s*.

MITFORD, J., *Letters*, 3*s*. 6*d*.

——— MISS, *Our Village*, illus. 5*s*.

MODY, MRS., *German Literature*, outlines, 1*s*.

MOFFATT, W., *Land and Work*, 5*s*.

MOINET. See Preachers.

MOLLETT. See Great Artists.

MOLONEY, J. A., *With Captain Stairs to Katanga*, 8*s*. 6*d*.

MONKHOUSE. See G. Artists.

Montaigne's Essays, revised by J. Hain Friswell, 2*s*. 6*d*.

MONTBARD (G.), *Among the Moors*, 16*s*. ; ed. *de Luxe*, 63*s*.

MOORE, J.M., *New Zealand for Emigrant, Invalid, and Tourist*, 5*s*.

MORLEY, HENRY, *English Literature in the Reign of Victoria*, 2*s*. 6*d*.

MORSE, E. S., *Japanese Homes*, new edit. 10*s*. 6*d*.

MORTEN,H., *Hospital Life*, 1*s*.

——— *Illnesses & Accidents*, 2*s*. 6*d*.

——— & GETHEN, *Tales of the Children's Ward*, 3*s*. 6*d*.

MORTIMER, J., *Chess Player's Pocket-Book*, new edit. 1*s*.

MOSS, F. J., *Great South Sea, Atolls and Islands*, 8*s*. 6*d*.

MOTTI, PIETRO, *Elementary Russian Grammar*, 2*s*. 6*d*.

——— *Russian Conversation Grammar*, 5*s*. ; Key, 2*s*.

MOULE, H.C.G. See Preachers.

MOUTON, E., *Adventures of a Breton Boy*, 5*s*.

MOXLY, *West India Sanatorium ; Barbados*, 3*s*. 6*d*.

MOZART. See Gr. Musicians.

MULERTT, H., *Gold Fish Culture*, 5*s*.

MULLER,E. See Low's Standard Books.

MULLIN, J.P., *Moulding and Pattern Making*, 12*s*. 6*d*.

MULREADY. See Gt. Artists.

MURDOCH, *Ayame San*, a Japanese Romance, 30*s*. nett.

MURILLO. See Great Artists.

MURPHY, *Beyond the Ice*, from Farleigh's Diary, 3*s*. 6*d*.

MUSGRAVE, MRS. See Low's Standard Novels.

My Comforter, &c., Religious Poems, 2*s*. 6*d*.

Napoleon I. See Bayard Series.

Napoleon I., Decline and Fall of.
See Wolseley.

NELSON, WOLFRED, *Panama,*
the Canal, &c., 6s.

Nelson's Words and Deeds, 3s. 6d.

NETHERCOTE, *Pytchley
Hunt,* 8s. 6d.

New Zealand, chromos, by Barraud, text by Travers, 168s.

NICHOLS, W. L., *Quantocks,*
5s.; large paper, 10s. 6d.

NICOLS, A., *Salmonidæ,* 5s.

Nineteenth Century, a Monthly
Review, 2s. 6d. per No.

NISBET, HUME, *Life and
Nature Studies,* illustrated, 6s.

NIVEN,R.,*Angler's Lexicon,*6s.

NORMAN, C. B., *Corsairs of
France,* 18s.

NORMAN, J. H., *Monetary
Systems of the World,* 10s. 6d.

—— *Ready Reckoner of Foreign
and Colonial Exchanges,* 2s. 6d.

NORWAY, 50 photogravures
by Paul Lange, text by E. J.
Goodman, 52s. 6d. nett.

—— S., *How Martin Drake,*
5s. and 2s. 6d.

NOTTAGE, C. G., *In Search
of a Climate,* illust. 25s.

Nugent's French Dictionary, 3s.

O'BRIEN, *Fifty Years of Concession to Ireland,* 2 vols. 32s.

OGAWA, *Open-Air Life in
Japan,* 15s. nett ; *Out of doors Life
in Japan,* 12s. nett.

OGDEN, J., *Fly-tying,* 2s. 6d.

Ohrwalder's Ten Years' Captivity ; Mahdi's Camp, 6s. & 2s. 6d.

Orient Line Guide, fourth edit.
by W. J. Loftie, 3s. 6d.

ORTOLI, *Evening Tales,* done
into English by J. C. Harris, 6s.

ORVIS, C. F., *Fly Fishing,*
with coloured plates, 12s. 6d.

OSBORN, H. S., *Prospector's
Guide,* 8s. 6d.

OTTO, E., *French and German
Grammars, &c.* List on application.

Our Little Ones in Heaven, 5s.

Out of Doors Life in Japan,
Burton's photos. See Ogawa.

Out of School at Eton, 2s. 6d.

OVERBECK. See Great Artists.

OWEN, *Marine Insurance,* 15s.

PAGE, T. N., *Marse Chan,*
illust. 6s.

—— *Meh Lady,* a Story of Old
Virginian Life, illus. 6s.

PALAZ, A., *Industrial Photometry,* 12s. 6d.

PALGRAVE, R. F. D. *Chairman's Handbook,* 12th edit. 2s.

—— *Oliver Cromwell,* 10s. 6d.

PALLISER, MRS. BURY, *China
Collector's Companion,* 5s.

—— *History of Lace,* n. ed. 21s.

PANTON,*Homes of Taste,*2s.6d

PARKE, T. H., *Emin Pasha
Relief Expedition,* 21s.

—— *Health in Africa,* 5s.

PARKER, E. H., *Chinese Account of the Opium War,* 1s. 6d.

—— J., *Thermo Dynamics,*
10s. 6d.

PARKS, LEIGHTON, *Winning
of the Soul, &c.,* sermons, 3s. 6d.

*Parliamentary Pictures and
Personalities* (from the *Graphic*),
illust., 5s. ; ed. de luxe, 21s. nett.

PATTERSON, CAPT., *Navigator's Pocket Book,* 5s.

PEACH, *Annals of Swainswick,*
near Bath, 10s. 6d.

Peel. See Prime Ministers.

PELLESCHI, G., *Gran Chaco
of the Argentine Republic,* 8s. 6d.

PEMBERTON, C.,*Tyrol,*1s.4d.

PENDLETON, L. See Low's Standard Novels.
PENNELL, *Fishing Tackle*, 2s.
—— *Sporting Fish*, 15s. & 30s.
Penny Postage Jubilee, 1s.
Pensions for all at Sixty, 6d.
PERL, H., *Venice*, 28s.
PHELPS, E. S., *Struggle for Immortality*, 5s.
—— SAMUEL, *Life*, by W. M. Phelps & Forbes-Robertson, 12s.
PHILBRICK, F. A., AND WESTOBY, *Post and Telegraph Stamps*, 10s. 6d.
PHILLIMORE, C. M., *Italian Literature*, new. edit. 3s. 6d.
——See also Gt. Artists, *Fra An.*
PHILLIPS, L. P., *Dictionary of Biographical Reference*, n.e. 25s.
—— E., *How to Become a Journalist*, 2s. 6d.
—— W., *Law of Insurance*, 2 vols. 73s. 6d.
PHILPOT, H. J., *Diabetes*, 5s.
—— *Diet Tables*, 1s. each.
PICKARD, S. F., *Whittier's Life*, 2 vols., 18s.
PIERCE, *Memoir of C. Sumner*, 2 vols., 36s.
Playtime Library, 2s. 6d. each.
Charles, Where is Fairy Land?
Humphreys, Little Britons.
Huntingdon, Squire's Nieces.
PLUNKETT (solid geometry) *Orthographic Projection*, 2s. 6d.
POE, E. A., *Raven*, ill. by G. Doré, 63s.
Poems of the Inner Life, 5s.
Poetry of the Anti-Jacobin, 7s. 6d.
POPE, W. H., *Fly Fisher's Register*, 4s.
—— F. L., *Electric Telegraph*, 12s. 6d.
PORCHER, A., *Juvenile French Plays*, with Notes, 1s.

PORTER, NOAH, *Memoir*, 8s. 6d.
Portraits of Racehorses, 4 vols. 126s.
POSSELT, *Structure of Fibres, Yarns and Fabrics*, 63s.
—— *Textile Design*, illust. 28s.
POTTER, F. S., *Walter Gaydon*, 5s.
POYNTER. See Illustrated Text Books.
Preachers of the Age, 3s. 6d. ea.
Living Theology, by His Grace the Archbishop of Canterbury.
The Conquering Christ, by Rev. A. Maclaren.
Verbum Crucis, by the Bishop of Derry.
Ethical Christianity, by Hugh P. Hughes.
Knowledge of God, by the Bishop of Wakefield.
Light and Peace, by H. R. Reynolds.
Journey of Life, by W. J. Knox-Little.
Messages to the Multitude, by C. H. Spurgeon.
Christ is All, by H. C. G. Moule, M.A.
Plain Words on Great Themes, by J. O. Dykes.
Children of God, by E. A. Stuart.
Christ in the Centuries, by A. M. Fairbairn.
Agoniae Christi, by Dr. Lefroy.
The Transfigured Sackcloth, by W. L. Watkinson.
The Gospel of Work, by the Bishop of Winchester.
Vision and Duty, by C. A. Berry.
The Burning Bush; Sermons, by the Bishop of Ripon.
Good Cheer of Jesus Christ, by C. Moinet, M.A.
A Cup of Cold Water, by J. Morlais Jones.
The Religion of the Son of Man, by E. J. Gough, M.A.
PRICE, *Arctic Ocean to Yellow Sea*, illust., new ed., 7s. 6d.

Prime Ministers, a series of political biographies, edited by Stuart J. Reid, 3s. 6d. each.

Earl of Beaconsfield, by J. Anthony Froude.

Viscount Melbourne, by Henry Dunckley ("*Verax*").

Sir Robert Peel, by Justin McCarthy.

Viscount Palmerston, by the Marquis of Lorne.

Lord John Russell, by Stuart J. Reid.

Right Hon. W. E. Gladstone, by G. W. E. Russell.

Earl of Aberdeen, by Baron Stanmore.

Marquis of Salisbury, by H. D. Traill.

Earl of Derby, by G. Saintsbury.

** An edition, limited to 250 copies, medium 8vo, half vellum, cloth sides, gilt top, 9 vols. 4l. 4s. nett.

Prince Maskiloff. See Low's Standard Novels.

Prince of Nursery Playmates, new edit. 2s. 6d.

PRITT, T. N., *North Country Flies*, coloured plates, 10s. 6d.

Publisher's Circular, weekly, 1½d.

Purcell. See Great Musicians.

PYLE, HOWARD, *Robin Hood*, 10s. 6d.

QUILTER, HARRY, *Giotto, Life, &c.* 15s. See also Great Artists.

RAFTER & BAKER, *Sewage Disposal*, 24s.

RAIFE, R., *Sheik's White Slave*, 6s.

RAPHAEL. See Great Artists.

REDFORD, *Sculpture*. See Illustrated Text-books.

REDGRAVE, *Century of English Painters*, new ed., 7s. 6d.

REED, T. B. See Low's St.Bks.

REID, MAYNE, CAPTAIN. See Low's Standard Books.

REID, STUART J. See Prime Min.

Remarkable Bindings in British Museum; 73s. 6d. and 63s.

REMBRANDT. See Gr. Artists.

REYNOLDS. See Gr. Artists.

REMUSAT, MADAME DE, *Memoirs*, 7s. 6d.

—— HENRY R. See Preachers.

RICHARDS, J. W., *Aluminium*, new edit. 21s.

RICHTER, *Italian Art in the National Gallery*, 42s.

—— See also Great Artists.

RIDDELL, MRS. J. H. See Low's Standard Novels.

RIPON, BP. OF. See Preachers.

RIVIÈRE, J., *Recollections*, 3s. 6d.

ROBERTS, LORD, *Rise of Wellington*, 3s. 6d.

—— W., *English Bookselling*, earlier history, 3s. 6d.

ROBERTSON, DR. AL., *Fra Paolo Sarpi*, 6s.

—— *Count Campello*, 5s.

ROBIDA, A., *Toilette*, coloured plates, 7s. 6d.; new ed. 3s. 6d.

ROBINSON, H. P., *Works on Photography*. List on application.

ROBINSON, PHIL., *Noah's Ark*, n. ed. 3s. 6d.

—— *Sinners & Saints*, 10s. 6d.; new ed. 3s. 6d.

—— See also Low's Stan. Ser.

—— SERJ., *Wealth and its Sources*, 5s.

—— J. R., *Princely Chandos*, illust., 12s. 6d.

—— *Last Earls of Barrymore*, 12s. 6d.

—— "*Old Q.*" 7s. 6d. and 21s.

—— "*Romeo*" *Coates*, 7s. 6d.

ROCKSTRO, *History of Music*, new ed. 14s.

RODRIGUES, *Panama Can.*, 5s.

ROE, E. P. See Low's St. Ser.

ROLFE, *Pompeii*, n. ed., 7s. 6d., with Photos, 14s.

ROMNEY. See Great Artists.

ROOPER, G., *Thames and Tweed*, 2s. 6d.

ROSE, J., *Mechanical Drawing Self-Taught*, 16s.

—— *Key to Engines*, 8s. 6d.

—— *Practical Machinist*, new ed. 12s. 6d.

—— *Steam Engines*, 31s. 6d.

—— *Steam Boilers*, 12s. 6d.

Rose Library. Per vol. 1s., unless the price is given.

Alcott (L. M.) Eight Cousins, 2s.

—— Jack and Jill, 2s.

—— Jimmy's cruise in the *Pinafore*, 2s. ; cloth, 3s. 6d.

—— Little Women.

—— Little Women Wedded ; Nos. 4 and 5 in 1 vol. cloth, 3s. 6d.

—— Little Men, 2s. ; cl. gt., 3s. 6d.

—— Old-fashioned Girls, 2s.; cloth, 3s. 6d.

—— Rose in Bloom, 2s. ; cl. 3s. 6d.

—— Silver Pitchers.

—— Under the Lilacs, 2s.; cl.3s.6d.

—— Work, 2 vols. in 1, cloth, 3s.6d.

Stowe (Mrs.) Pearl of Orr's Island.

—— Minister's Wooing.

—— We and Our Neighbours, 2s.

—— My Wife and I, 2s.

—— Dred, 2s. ; cl. gt., 3s. 6d.

Dodge (Mrs.) Hans Brinker, 1s. ; cloth, 5s. ; 3s. 6d. ; 2s. 6d.

Holmes, Guardian Angel, cloth, 2s.

Carleton (W.) City Ballads, 2 vols. in 1, cloth gilt, 2s. 6d.

—— Legends, 2 vols. in 1, cloth gilt, 2s. 6d.

—— Farm Ballads, 6d. and 9d. ; 3 vols. in 1, cloth gilt, 3s. 6d.

—— Farm Festivals, 3 vols. in 1, cloth gilt, 3s. 6d.

—— Farm Legends, 3 vols. in 1, cloth gilt, 3s. 6d.

Biart, Bernagius' Clients, 2 vols.

Howells, Undiscovered Country.

Rose Library—Continued.

Clay (C. M.) Baby Rue.

—— Story of Helen Troy.

Whitney, Hitherto, 2 vols. 3s. 6d.

Fawcett (E.) Gentleman of Leisure

Butler, Nothing to Wear.

ROSSETTI. See Wood.

ROSSINI, &c. See Great Mus.

Rothschilds, by J. Reeves, 7s. 6d.

Roughing it after Gold, by Rux, new edit. 1s.

ROUSSELET. See Low's Standard Books.

Royal Naval Exhibition, illus. 1s.

RUBENS. See Great Artists.

RUSSELL, G.W. E., *Gladstone*. See Prime Ministers.

—— H., *Ruin of Soudan*, 21s.

—— W. CLARK, *Mrs. Dines' Jewels*, cloth, 2s. 6d., boards, 2s.

—— *Nelson's Words and Deeds*, 3s. 6d.

—— *Sailor's Language*, 3s. 6d.

—— See also Low's Standard Novels.

—— W. HOWARD, *Prince of Wales' Tour*, ill. 52s. 6d.

Russia's March towards India, by an Indian Officer, 2 vols., 16s.

Russian Art, 105s.

St. Dunstan's Library, 3s. 6d. each.

1. A Little Sister to the Wilderness, by L. Bell.

2. Corona of the Nantahalas, by L. Pendleton.

3. Two Mistakes, by Sydney Christian.

4. Love Affairs of an Old Maid, by L. Bell.

Saints and their Symbols, 3s. 6d.

SAINTSBURY, G., *Earl of Derby*. See Prime Ministers.

SALISBURY, LORD. See Prime Ministers.

SAMUELS. See Low's Standard Series.

SAMUELSON, James, *Greece, her Condition and Progress*, 5s.
SANBORN, KATE, *A Truthful Woman in S. California*, 3s. 6d.
SANDARS, *German Primer*, 1s.
SANDLANDS, *How to Develop Vocal Power*, 1s.
SAUER, *European Commerce*, 5s.
—— *Italian Grammar* (Key, 2s.), 5s.
—— *Spanish Dialogues*, 2s. 6d.
—— *Spanish Grammar* (Key, 2s.), 5s.
—— *Spanish Reader*, 3s. 6d.
SCHAACK, *Anarchy*, 16s.
SCHERER, *Essays in English Literature*, by G. Saintsbury, 6s.
SCHILLER'S *Prosa*, 2s. 6d.
SCHUBERT. See Great Mus.
SCHUMANN. See Great Mus.
SCHWAB, *Age of the Horse ascertained by the teeth*, 2s. 6d.
SCHWEINFURTH, *Heart of Africa*, 2 vols., 3s. 6d. each.
Scientific Education of Dogs, 6s.
SCOTT, LEADER, *Renaissance of Art in Italy*, 31s. 6d.
—— See also Great Artists and Illust. Text Books.
—— SIR GILBERT, *Autobiography*, 18s.
Scribner's Magazine, monthly, 1s.; half-yearly volumes, 8s. 6d.
Sea Stories. See Russell in Low's Standard Novels.
SENIOR, W., *Near and Far*, 2s.
—— *Waterside Sketches*, 1s.
SEVERN, JOSEPH, *Life, Letters, and Friendships*, by Sharp, 21s.
Shadow of the Rock, 2s. 6d.
SHAFTESBURY. See English Philosophers.
SHAKESPEARE, ed. by R. G. White, 3 vols. 36s.; 1. paper, 63s.
—— *Annals; Life & Work*, 2s.

SHAKESPEARE, *Hamlet*, 1603, 7s. 6d.
—— *Heroines*, by living painters, 105s.
—— *Home and Haunts of*, 315s.
—— *Macbeth*, with etchings, 105s. and 52s. 6d.
—— *Songs and Sonnets.* See Choice Editions.
SHALER, N. S., *The U.S. of America*, 36s.
SHEPHERD, *British School of Painting*, 2nd edit. 5s. and 1s.
SHERMAN, GENL., *Letters*, 16s.
SHUMWAY, *Tuberculosis*, 3s. 6d. nett.
SIDNEY, SIR PHILIP, *Arcadia*, new ed., 6s.
SIMSON, *Ecuador and the Putumayor River*, 8s. 6d.
SKOTTOWE, *Hanoverian Kings*, new edit. 3s. 6d.
SLOANE, T. O., *Home Experiments in Science*, 6s.
SLOANE, W. M., *French War and the Revolution*, 7s. 6d.
SMITH, CHARLES W., *Theories and Remedies for Depression in Trade*, &c., 2s.
—— *Commercial Gambling the Cause of Depression*, 3s. 6d.
—— G., *Assyria*, 18s
—— *Chaldean Account of Genesis*, new edit. by Sayce, 18s.
—— SYDNEY, *Life*, 21s.
——T. ASSHETON, *Reminiscences* by Sir J. E. Wilmot, 2s. 6d. and 2s.
—— T. ROGER. See Illustrated Text Books.
—— W. A., *Shepherd Smith, the Universalist*, 8s. 6d.
—— HAMILTON, and LEGROS' *French Dictionary*, 2 vols. 16s., 21s., and 22s.
SMITT, PROF., *Scandinavian Fishes*, 2 Parts, 252s. nett.

SNOWDEN (J. K.), *Tales of the Yorkshire Wolds*, 3s. 6d.

SOMERSET, *Our Village Life*, with coloured plates, 5s.

SPIERS, *French Dictionary*, new ed., 2 vols. 18s., half bound, 21s.

SPRY. See Low's Standard Library of Travel.

SPURGEON, C. H. See Preachers.

STANLEY, H. M., *Congo*, new ed., 2 vols., 21s.

—— *Coomassie&Magdala*,3s.6d.

—— *Early Travels*, 2 vols., 12s. 6d.

—— *Emin's Rescue*, 1s.

—— *In Darkest Africa*, 2 vols., 42s.; new edit. 1 vol. 10s. 6d.

—— *My Dark Companions and their Strange Stories*, illus. 7s. 6d.

—— See also Low's Standard Library and Low's Stand. Books.

START, *Exercises in Mensuration*, 8d.

STEPHENS. See Great Artists.

STERNE. See Bayard Series.

STERRY, J. ASHBY, *Cucumber Chronicles*, 5s.

STEUART, J. A., *Letters to Living Authors*, new edit. 2s. 6d.; édit. de luxe, 10s. 6d.

—— See also Low's Standard Novels.

STEVENI (W. B.). *Through Famine-Stricken Russia*, 3s. 6d.

STEVENS, J. W., *Leather Manufacture*, illust. 18s.

STEWART, DUGALD, *Outlines of Moral Philosophy*, 3s. 6d.

STOCKTON, F. R., *Ardis Claverden*, 6s.

—— *Clocks of Rondaine*, 7s. 6d.

—— *Mrs. Lecks*, 1s.

—— *The Dusantes*, a sequel to *Mrs. Lecks*, 1s.

STOCKTON, F. R., *Personally Conducted* (*tour in Europe*), illust. 7s. 6d.

—— *Rudder Grangers Abroad*, 2s. 6d.

—— *Schooner Merry Chanter*, 2s. 6d. and 1s.

—— *Squirrel Inn*, illust. 6s.

—— *Story of Viteau*, 5s., 3s.6d.

—— *Three Burglars*, 2s. & 1s.

—— See also Low's Standard Novels.

STODDARD, W. O., *Beyond the Rockies*, 7s. 6d.

STOKER, BRAM, *Under the Sunset*, Christmas Stories, 6s.

—— *Snake's Pass*, 3s. 6d.

STORER, F. H., *Agriculture and Chemistry*, 2 vols., 25s.

Stories from Scribner, illust., 6 vols., transparent wrapper. 1s. 6d. each; cloth, top gilt, 2s. each.

1. Of New York.	4. Of the Sea.
2. Of the Railway.	5. Of the Army.
3. Of the South.	6. Of Italy.

Story of My Two Wives, 3s. 6d.

STOWE, MRS., *Flowers and Fruit from Her Writings*, 3s. 6d.

—— *Life . . . her own Words . . . Letters, &c.*, 15s.

—— *Life*, for boys and girls, by S. A. Tooley, 5s., 2s. 6d. and 2s.

—— *Little Foxes*, cheap edit. 1s.; also 4s. 6d.

—— *Minister's Wooing*, 2s.

—— *Pearl of Orr's Island*, 3s. 6d. and 1s.

—— *Uncle Tom's Cabin*, with 126 new illust. 2 vols. 16s.

—— See also Low's Standard Novels and Low's Standard Series.

STRACHAN, J., *New Guinea Explorations*, 12s.

STRANAHAN, *French Painting*, 21s.

STRICKLAND, F., *Engadine*, new edit. 5s.

STRONGE, S. E., & EAGAR, *English Grammar*, 3s.

STUART, E. A. See Preachers.

—— Esmé, *Claude's Island*, 6s.

STUTFIELD, *El Maghreb*, 8s. 6d.

SUMNER, C., *Memoir*, vols. iii., iv., 36s.

Sylvanus Redivivus, 10s. 6d. ; new ed., 3s. 6d.

SYNGE, G. M., *Ride through Wonderland*, 3s. 6d.

SZCZEPANSKI, *Technical Literature*, a directory, 2s.

TAINE, H. A., *Origines*, I. Ancient Regime and French Revolution, 3 vols., 16s. ea. ; Modern, I. and II., 16s. ea.

TAUNTON, *Celebrated Race-horses*, 126s.

—— *Equine Celebrities*, 25s.

TAYLER, J., *Beyond the Bustle*, 6s.

TAYLOR, Hannis, *English Constitution*, 18s.

—— Mrs. Bayard, *Letters to a Young Housekeeper*, 5s.

—— R. L., *Analysis Tables*, 1s.

—— *Chemistry*, n. ed., 2s.

—— *Students' Chemistry*, 5s.

—— and S. PARRISH, *Chemical Problems, with Solutions*, 2s.6d.

Techno-Chemical Receipt Book, by Braunt and Wahl, 10s. 6d.

THANET, *Stories of a Western Town* (United States), 6s.

THAUSING, *Malt & Beer*, 45s.

THEAKSTON, *British Angling Flies*, illust., 5s.

Thomas à Kempis Birthday-Book, 3s. 6d.

—— *Daily Text-Book*, 2s. 6d.

THOMAS, Bertha, *House on the Scar, Tale of South Devon*, 6s.

THOMSON, Joseph. See Low's Stan. Lib. and Low's Stan. Novs.

—— W., *Algebra*, 5s. ; without Answers, 4s. 6d. ; Key, 1s. 6d.

THORNDYKE, Sherman's, *Letters*, 16s.

THORNTON, W. Pugin, *Heads, and what they tell us*, 1s.

THOREAU, H. D., *Life*, 2s. 6d.

THORODSEN, J P., *Lad and Lass*, 6s.

TILESTON, Mary W., *Daily Strength*, 5s. and 3s. 6 l.

TINTORETTO. See Gr. Art.

TITIAN. See Great Artists.

TODD, Alphaeus, *Parliamentary Government in England*, 2 vols., 15s.

—— Eyre, *Anne of Argyle*, 6s.

—— M. L., *Total Eclipses*, 3s. 6d.

TOLSTOI, A. K., *The Terrible Czar, a Romance of the time of Ivan the Terrible*, new ed. 2s. 6d.

TOMPKINS, *Through David's Realm*, illust. by author, 5s.

TOURGEE. See Low's Standard Novels.

TRACY, A., *Rambles Through Japan without a Guide*, 6s.

TRAILL. See Prime Ministers.

—— Mrs. C. P., *Pearls and Pebbles*. 8s. 6d.

TURNER, J. M. W. See Gr. Artists.

Twentieth Century Practice of Medicine, 20 vols., 420s.

TYACKE, Mrs., *How I shot my Bears*, illust., 7s. 6d.

TYTLER, Sarah. See Low's Standard Novels.

UPTON, II., *Dairy Farming*, 2s.

Valley Council, by P. Clarke, 6s.

VANDYCK and HALS. See Great Artists.

In all Departments of Literature. 29

VAN DYKE, J. C., *Art for Art's Sake*, 7s. 6d.

VANE, Denzil, *Lynn's Court Mystery*, 1s.

—— See also Low's St. Nov.

Vane, Young Sir Harry, 18s.

VAN HARE, *Showman's Life*, Fifty Years, new ed., 2s. 6d.

VELAZQUEZ. See Gr. Artists.

—— and MURILLO, by C. B. Curtis, with etchings, 31s. 6d.

VERNE, J., *Works by.* See page 31.

Vernet and Delaroche. See Great Artists.

VERSCHUUR, G., *At the Antipodes*, 7s. 6d.

VINCENT, Dr. C., *Chant-book Companion*, 2s. and 4s.

—— Mrs. Howard, 40,000 *Miles over Land and Water*, 2 vols. 21s.; also 3s. 6d.

—— *Newfoundland to Cochin China*, new ed. 3s. 6d.

—— *China to Peru*, 7s. 6d.

WAGNER. See Gr. Musicians.

WAHNSCHAFFE, *Scientific Examination of Soil*, by Braunt, 8s. 6d.

WAKEFIELD, Bishop of. See Preachers.

WALFORD, Mrs. L. B. See Low's Standard Novels.

WALL, *Tombs of the Kings of England*, 21s.

WALLACE, L., *Ben Hur*, 2s.

—— Professor, *Australia*, 21s.

WALLACK, L., *Memoirs*, 7s. 6d.

WALLER, *Silver Sockets*, 6s.

WALTON, Iz., *Angler*, Lea and Dove edit. by R. B. Marston, with photos., 210s. and 105s.

—— T. H., *Coal-mining*, 25s.

WARBURTON, Col., *Race-horse, How to Buy, &c.*, 6s.

WARDROP, Ol., *Kingdom of Georgia*, 14s.

WARNER, C. D. See Low's Stand. Novels and Low's Stand. Series.

WARREN, W. F., *Paradise Found*, illust. 12s. 6d.

WATKINSON. See Preachers.

WATSON, J., *Handbook for Farmers*, 4s. 6d.

—— J. B., *Swedish Revolution*, 12s.

WATTEAU. See Great Artists.

WEBER. See Great Musicians.

WELLINGTON. See Bayard Series.

—— *Rise of.* See Roberts.

WELLS, H. P., *Salmon Fisherman*, 6s.

—— *Fly-rods & Tackle*, 10s. 6d.

WENZEL, *Chemical Products of the German Empire*, 25s.

WESTGARTH, *Australasian Progress*, 12s.

WESTOBY, *Postage Stamps*, 5s.

WESTON, J., *Night in the Woods*, 3s. 6d.

Whincop's Pocket Chess Board, 5s.

WHITE, R. Grant, *England Without and Within*, 10s. 6d.

—— *Every-day English*, 10s. 6d.

—— *Studies in Shakespeare*, 10s. 6d.

—— *Words and their Uses*, new edit. 5s.

—— W., *Our English Homer*, Shakespeare and his Plays, 6s.

WHITNEY, Mrs. See Low's Standard Series.

WHITTIER, St. Gregory's Guest, 5s.

—— *Life, by Pickard*, 18s.

—— *Text and Verse for Every Day in the Year*, selections, 1s. 6d.

WILCOX, Marrion. See Low's Standard Novels.

WILKIE. See Great Artists.
WILLS, *Persia as it is,* 8s. 6d.
WILSON, *Health for the People*
7s. 6d.
—— Mrs. R., *Land of the Tui,*
7s. 6d.
—— H. W., *Ironclad Warfare.*
WINCHESTER, Bishop of.
See Preachers of the Age.
WINDER, *Lost in Africa.* See
Low's Standard Books.
WINGATE. See Ohrwalder.
WINSOR, J., *Columbus,* 21s.
—— *Cartier to Frontenac,* 15s.
—— *History of America,* 8 vols.
per vol. 30s. and 63s.
—— *Mississippi Basin,* 21s.
With Havelock from Allahabad,
2s. 6d.
WITTHAUS, *Chemistry,* 16s.
WOLLASTON, A. N., *Anwar-
i-Suhali,* 15s.
—— *English-Persian Diction-
ary,* 31s. 6d.
—— *Half Hours with Muham-
mad,* 3s. 6d.
WOLSELEY, Lord, *Decline
and Fall of Napoleon,* 3s. 6d.
*Woman's Mission, Congress
Papers,* edited by the Baroness
Burdett-Coutts, 10s. 6d.

WOOD, Esther, *Dante Gabriel
Rossetti and the Pre-Raphaelite
Movement,* with illustrations from
Rossetti's paintings, 12s. 6d.
—— Sir Evelyn, *Life,* by
Williams, 14s.
*Cavalry in the Waterloo Cam-
paign,* 3s. 6d.
WOOLSEY, *Communism and
Socialism,* 7s. 6d.
—— *International Law,* 18s.
—— *Political Science,* 2 v. 30s.
WOOLSON, C. Fenimore.
See Low's Standard Novels.
WORDSWORTH. See Choice.
Wreck of the "Grosvenor."
See Low's Standard Novels.
WRIGHT, H., *Friendship of
God,* 6s.
—— T., *Town of Cowper,* 3s. 6d.
WRIGLEY, *Algiers Illustrated,*
100 views in photogravure, 45s.
Written to Order, 6s.
YEATS, S. LEVETT, *Honour
of Savelli,* 6s.
YORKE DAVIES, Dr., *Health
and Condition,* 3s. 6d.
Ziemssen's Medicine, £18 18s.
YOUNGHUSBAND, Capt. G.
J., *On Short Leave to Japan,* 6s.

*** Messrs. SAMPSON LOW, MARSTON & CO., Ltd., are the publishers of a number of works in the Eastern Languages —Hindustani, Bengali, Sanscrit, Persian, Arabic, &c.—which were formerly issued by Messrs. W. H. ALLEN & Co., Ltd.

Many of these books are used as Text-books in the Examinations for the Indian Civil Service and the Indian Staff Corps, also as Class-books in Colleges and Schools in India.

Complete Catalogue of Works in the Oriental Languages forwarded on application.

London: SAMPSON LOW, MARSTON & COMPANY, Ltd.;
St. Dunstan's House, Fetter Lane, Fleet Street, E.C.

BOOKS BY JULES VERNE.

LARGE CROWN 8vo. WORKS.	Containing 350 to 800 pp. and from 50 to 100 full-page illustrations.		Containing the whole of the text with some illustrations.	
	Handsome cloth binding, gilt edges.	Plainer binding, plain edges.	Cloth binding, gilt edges, smaller type.	Limp cloth.
	s. d.	s. d.	s. d.	s. d.
20,000 Leagues under the Sea. Parts I. and II.	10 6	5 0	3 6	2 0
Hector Servadac	10 6	5 0	3 6	2 0
The Fur Country	10 6	5 0	3 6	2 0
The Earth to the Moon and a Trip round it	10 6	5 0	{ 2 vols., 2s. ea.	2 vols., 1s. ea. }
Michael Strogoff	10 6	5 0	3 6	2 0
Dick Sands, the Boy Captain	10 6	5 0	3 6	2 0
Five Weeks in a Balloon	7 6	2 6	2 0	1 0
Adventures of Three Englishmen and Three Russians	7 6	3 6	2 0	1 0
Round the World in Eighty Days	7 6	3 6	2 0	1 0
A Floating City	7 6	{ 3 6	{ 2 0	1 0
The Blockade Runners		& 2 6	2 0	1 0
Dr. Ox's Experiment	—	—	2 0	1 0
A Winter amid the Ice	—	—	2 0	1 0
Survivors of the "Chancellor"	7 6	3 6	{ 3 6	{ 2 0
Martin Paz			2 0	1 0
The Mysterious Island, 3 vols.:—	22 6	10 6	6 0	3 0
I. Dropped from the Clouds	7 6	3 6	2 0	1 0
II. Abandoned	7 6	3 6	2 0	1 0
III. Secret of the Island	7 6	3 6	2 0	1 0
The Child of the Cavern	7 6	3 6	2 0	1 0
The Begum's Fortune	7 6	3 6	2 0	1 0
The Tribulations of a Chinaman	7 6	3 6	2 0	1 0
The Steam House, 2 vols.:—				
I. Demon of Cawnpore	7 6	3 6	2 0	1 0
II. Tigers and Traitors	7 6	3 6	2 0	1 0
The Giant Raft, 2 vols.:—				
I. 800 Leagues on the Amazon	7 6	3 6	2 0	1 0
II. The Cryptogram	7 6	3 6	2 0	1 0
The Green Ray	5 0	3 6	2 0	1 0
Godfrey Morgan	7 6	3 6	2 0	1 0
Keraban the Inflexible:—				
I. Captain of the "Guidara"	7 6	3 6	2 0	1 0
II. Scarpante the Spy	7 6	3 6	2 0	1 0
The Archipelago on Fire	7 6	3 6	2 0	1 0
The Vanished Diamond	7 6	3 6	2 0	1 0
Mathias Sandorf	10 6	5 0	3 6	2 vols 1 0 each
Lottery Ticket	7 6	3 6	2 0	1 0
The Clipper of the Clouds	7 6	3 6	2 0	1 0
North against South	7 6	3 6	—	2 vols 1 0 each
Adrift in the Pacific	6 0	2 6		
The Flight to France	7 6	3 6	2 0	1 0
The Purchase of the North Pole	6 0	2 6		
A Family without a Name	6 0	2 6		
Cesar Cascabel	6 0	2 6		

Mistress Branican ; Castle of the Carpathians ; Foundling Mick ; Captain Antifer ; Screw Island (*in the press*), 6s. only.

* *Special issue in eight cases of five books each, in a box, 4s. per box.*
CELEBRATED TRAVELS AND TRAVELLERS. 3 vols. 8vo, 600 pp., 100 full-page illustrations, 7s. 6d. gilt edges, 9s. each :—(1) THE EXPLORATION OF THE WORLD. (2) THE GREAT NAVIGATORS OF THE EIGHTEENTH CENTURY. (3) THE GREAT EXPLORERS OF THE NINETEENTH CENTURY.

www.ingramcontent.com/pod-product-compliance
Lightning Source LLC
Chambersburg PA
CBHW030602270326
41927CB00007B/1021